# Secrets of World Changers

## How to Achieve Lasting Influence as a Leader

## Jeff Myers

BROADMAN
&HOLMAN
PUBLISHERS

Nashville, Tennessee

## Special thanks to:

The Summit Ministries team, especially David Noebel, Todd Cothran, Tom Eckbladt,
and Kevin Bywater for a wonderful program and for making my video coaching possible;
Jackie Myers, Allison Combs and Alana Toliver for their assistance and editing help
(and Jackie for being a great mom, too);
The great folks at Broadman & Holman, especially Matt Stewart and Greg Webster
for their partnering vision and spirit;
Most of all to Danielle for the hours of patience (twice now!)
—the world is already changed because of you; I love you.

Copyright © 2006 Jeff Myers

All rights reserved.
Printed in the United States of America

10-digit ISBN: 0805468838
13-digit ISBN: 9780805468830

Published by Broadman & Holman Publishers
Nashville, Tennessee

DEWEY: 248.834
SUBHD: CHRISTIAN LIFE/ MISSIONS

Scripture text is from The Holy Bible, *Holman Christian Standard Bible* ®, Copyright © 1999, 2000, 2001, 2002, 2003 by Holman Bible Publishers.
Other "Credits, Permissions, and Sources" are listed at the back of the book.

1 2 3 4 5   10  09  08  07  06

# CONTENTS

# What Is a Leader?

## CHAPTER AT A GLANCE

- Perhaps you have come to the kingdom…
- …For such a time as this.
- Why me?
- The kingdom upside down.
- Small people in a world of big problems.
- Becoming a world-changer.

## Perhaps You Have Come to the Kingdom…

You've probably never heard of Edward Kimball. He was a shoe clerk in Boston, Massachusetts whose only claim to fame is that he loved the Lord and taught a Sunday school class for boys. Yet Edward Kimball is responsible for millions upon millions of people coming to faith in Jesus Christ. How?

Kimball once invited a boy named Dwight Moody to his Sunday school class after which Moody trusted Christ and grew up to be one of America's greatest evangelists. Once Moody preached a sermon that caused a college pastor to renew his commitment to serve God. This pastor, F. B. Meyer, later discipled a student named J. Wilbur Chapman, who went to work for the Y.M.C.A. in North Carolina.

Through the Y.M.C.A., Chapman organized a series of evangelistic meetings with a former pro-baseball player named Billy Sunday. The events were so successful that Chapman organized another series of meetings for the following year, inviting Sunday's associate, Mordecai Ham, to preach. As Ham gave the invitation one evening, a lanky 16-year-old boy walked forward and trusted Christ. His name was Billy Graham. God used a shoe salesman, a man with only ordinary gifts, to start a chain reaction leading to one of the most powerful evangelistic ministries in history.

But at one time, Edward Kimball had a choice to make. What if he had remained silent about the Gospel out of embarrassment or fear? Fortunately, we don't have to contemplate the answer. Because Kimball was faithful, countless of people have heard the gospel through the ministry of Billy Graham.

## ...For Such a Time as This

In the video I told the story of a Hebrew girl named Esther who faced a choice much more difficult than whether or not to share her faith. She literally had to risk her life to confront evil, or allow her people to be killed.

Esther had become queen to Xerxes, the man who ruled most of the known world. Esther's cousin and guardian, Mordecai, uncovered a plot through which the king had unwittingly authorized the extermination of every one of God's chosen people, the Jews. Mordecai reasoned that Esther's high position might allow her to influence the king to avert the bloodbath, so he sent a message to Esther which read:

If you keep silent at this time, liberation and deliverance will come to the Jewish people from another place, but you and your father's house will be destroyed. Who knows, perhaps you have come to the kingdom for such a time as this. (Esther 4:14)

Think of it: Esther realized she was the only person who could save her people. She must have felt terribly frightened. If she confronted the king he might have her put to death. Still, she decided to take a stand. "I will go to the king," she said, "if I perish, I perish" (Esther 4:16). As a result of her courageous action, the Jewish people were saved. God used this solitary young girl to make an extraordinary difference for His people.

## Why Me?

In my *Great Communicators* study, I pointed out that Esther's savvy approach to the king made the most of her being in the right place at the right time. If you struggle with the fear of communication, *Great Communicators* will fill you with confidence and give you a step-by-step plan to conquer the fear of public speaking and move an audience to action. But it is important to note that Esther did not make her decision based on whether or not she thought she would succeed. *She made her decision based on what was right.* Esther acted in faith and surrendered the outcome to God.

Although Esther lived more than 2,500 years ago, in every age, in every nation, people must make the same choice that Esther made: speak up or remain silent, be part of the solution, or be part of the problem, be a bearer of light, or be content with darkness.

Every great hero of Scripture felt fear when God called them out. Their most common reaction was, "Why me?" That God through Scripture would tell us they were afraid is strangely comforting. It reminds us that even God's best can be fearful.

But I confess fear isn't my only reaction when God calls me out. I'm also filled with *disbelief*—why would an all-knowing God choose a knucklehead like me to carry out His plan? That's why it's important to understand the idea of servant leadership presented in the video lesson—that we make a difference from the bottom up rather than the top down.

Servant leadership isn't just a new-fangled way to get people to follow you. It is part of the fabric of the universe as God created it. God *always* chooses the weak to shame the strong, the small to confound the great. This makes no sense to the world. From the standpoint of mankind's sinful pride, God's plan is completely upside down.

## The Kingdom Upside Down

Along with millions of others, I was swept up in the *Lord of the Rings* frenzy several years ago. I read the books, saw the movies, and talked with many of my colleagues and students about the significance of J.R.R. Tolkien's work.

As I watched the movie trilogy, I enjoyed the talented actors and astonishing sets but found myself longing for more of the "history," the character development, dialogue, and poetry that made Tolkien's characters come alive in print.

Both in the books and in the movies, one thing was clear: the fate of Middle Earth rested on Frodo, a puny, terrified Hobbit. Frodo's mission was to destroy the One Ring before evil Sauron could use it to dominate the world.

Frodo didn't know what to do. He had never even been out of the Shire before, and powerful, wicked beings opposed him. Perhaps a wise wizard should have been chosen, or at least a mighty warrior elf. But it was Frodo who was given the seemingly hopeless task.

Tolkien's world enchants us because it is so…upside-down. The weak are chosen over the strong. Flawed, humble creatures achieve greatness. Great ones are brought low. I believe we find this world compelling, not because it is so foreign, but because it resonates with our deepest being—we know, in our hearts, that God intends to glorify Himself through our weakness.

Consider this: when God wants to do something really, really big, he always starts really, really small. In a universe of 50 billion galaxies, God apparently put organic life on only one planet, orbiting around one moderate-sized sun in a corner of just one of those galaxies.

Then He created only two people, Adam and Eve. They sinned, of course, jeopardizing the whole plan—or so it seemed. In pronouncing a curse on the serpent who had tempted Adam and Eve, God said the woman's offspring would strike the serpent's head (Genesis 3:15). This is a blessing in the midst of a curse: There will come one who will destroy the work of Satan in the world.

Most of the world was not paying attention when this serpent-crushing Savior arrived. He was born to a young girl who first nestled him in a feed trough and then raised him in Nazareth, a socially unimportant village in a seemingly worthless outpost of the Roman Empire. Yet that birth changed the world, and through the earthly ministry of Jesus, our lives take on a grand new level of significance. What was God thinking?

## Small People in a World of Big Problems

After September 11th, 2001, I became a different kind of parent. It wasn't so much that I saw my children's value in a new way. It's that I knew *they* saw *me* in a new way.

A few weeks after that tragic day, my son Graham, then age five, and my daughter Emma, then age three, were riding with me in our truck. Suddenly, Emma began worrying aloud about robbers breaking into our house. At the time we lived in a tightly knit

> "A ship in the harbor is safe, but that is not what ships are for."
>
> —John A. Shedd

> "I will put hostility between you and the woman, and between your seed and her seed. He will stike your head, and you will strike his heel."
>
> —Genesis 3:15

community with neighbors who were fiercely protective of one another and who believed strongly in the right to bear arms. No robbers even dared enter the neighborhood. But since I knew I couldn't explain this to my young daughter, I just listened.

Finally, Emma concluded the matter by asserting, "If robbers broke into our house, Papa would protect us." My chest swelled with pride until Graham broke in, "Yeah, but if they dropped an airplane on our house, *there is nothing he could do.*"

Graham is right of course. My abilities are limited, and it seems that my limitations far outweigh my abilities. If I allow myself to brood about it, I begin wondering how I can accomplish anything at all. Why would God choose me? Why not choose powerful, rich, suave individuals who could create change with a snap of their fingers? God's plan seems backwards.

## Becoming a World Changer

What ran through your mind when you first saw the title of this course, *Secrets of World Changers*? Perhaps you thought it would be an interesting study of people who made a difference. Such a study would give you confidence that at least *somebody* knows what's going on out there. But how did you feel when you realized the purpose of this study is to equip *you* for culture-shaping leadership?

Like me, maybe you feel weak and faint of heart when you contemplate your own role in changing our world for the better. It's hard to believe God sorted through millions of people and chose you and me for missions that no one else could accomplish. It's even harder to believe God chose us not in spite of our weaknesses, but *because* of them. "So because of Christ, I am pleased in weaknesses, in insults, in catastrophes, in persecutions, and in pressures. For when I am weak, then am I strong" (2 Corinthians 12:10).

God says in Isaiah 55:8, "For My thoughts are not your thoughts, and your ways are not my ways." God has invested us weaklings with an astounding source of strength—not for our own benefit, of course, but because living strong brings glory to Him.

As you work your way through this course, let this thought soak into your soul: God chooses *ordinary* people to accomplish the *extraordinary*. It's all part of His great plan for the ages.

I was considerng this one Sunday morning when a particularly courageous and faith-filled hymn caught my attention. The richness of the words penned by W. Y. Fullerton, and sung to the tune of "Londonderry Falls" soaked straight into my heart:

> I cannot tell how He will win the nations,
> How He will claim His earthly heritage.
> How satisfy the needs and aspirations
> Of east and west, of sinner and of sage.
> But this I know, all flesh shall see His glory,
> And He shall reap the harvest He has sown,
> And some glad day His sun shall shine in splendour
> When He the Saviour, Saviour of the world, is known.

You, and I, have been called to royal position for such a time as this, serving the King of all the vast universe. The vision, mission, motivation and planning skill we develop is not to serve ourselves but to be used in the service of this great quest, to spread the message of the Kingdom throughout the world.

The reality of how God uses people brings you to the valley of decision. Will you embrace your mission? I hope your answer is "yes," or at least "maybe." *Secrets of World Changers* may well be just the thing to light your fuse.

# Consider This

Take a few minutes, and jot down answers to these questions and statements. They will help you think through your personal concerns as you take on the challenge of being a world changer.

• **At the beginning of Chapter One, Dr. Myers mentions a man named Edward Kimball. What simple act did Mr. Kimball perform that changed the world?**

"Men are polished, through act and speech, each by each, as pebbles are smoothed on the rolling beach."

—John Townsend Trowbridge,
*A Home Idyl*

• **How would Edward Kimball have influenced the world if he had not performed that simple act?**

• **Write down a time when you took a stand for what was right:**

"God chooses ordinary people to accomplish the extraordinary. It's all part of His great plan for the ages."

—Jeff Myers

• **Write down a time when you did not take a stand for what was right but know that you should have:**

# Follow-Up Exercise

If it is true God has called you to a royal position for such a time as this, your life should reflect it. The word "testimony" means to bear witness to some fact. A testimony is more than telling others what God has done for you. It is the way your life demonstrates the power of God and the reality of living in Christ.

In a courtroom, witnesses give testimony under an oath by which they promise to tell the truth, the whole truth and nothing but the truth. Is there ever a time when Christians are not under oath to live the truth, the whole truth, and nothing but the truth about God?  [  ] **Yes**  [  ] **No**

In the Old Testament, God's testimony was His Word (Psalm 119:9-16). The children of Israel demonstrated that God had chosen them by carrying God's written words around with them in the ark (Exodus 25:16). Let's take a look at some ways Christians today can testify to the power of God.

**1. Look up the Scripture verses below, and fill in the blanks to see what God wants Christians to do to live their testimony every day.**

- 1 Peter 2:12—"Conduct yourselves _____ among the Gentiles, so that in a case where they speak against you as those who do evil, they may, by _____ your good works, glorify God in a day of visitation."

- Micah 6:8—"He has told you men what is good and what it is the Lord _____ of you: Only to act _____ to love _____ and  to walk _____ with God."

- 1 Peter 3:15—"...but set apart the _____ as Lord in your hearts, and always be ready to give a _____ to anyone who asks you for a _____ for the hope that is in you."

- 2 Timothy 2:24-25—"The Lord's slave must not _____, but must be gentle to _____, able to teach, and patient, instructing his opponents with _____. Perhaps God will grant them repentance to know the truth. Then they may come to their _____ and escape the Devil's trap, having been _____by him to do his will."

> "How can a young man keep his way pure? By keeping Your word.
>
> I have sought You with all my heart; don't let me wander from Your commands.
>
> I have treasured Your word in my heart so that I may not sin against You.
>
> Lord, may You be praised; teach me Your statutes.
>
> With my lips I proclaim all the judgments from Your mouth.
>
> I rejoice in the way revealed by Your decrees as much as in all riches.
>
> I will meditate on Your precepts and think about Your ways.
>
> I will delight in Your statutes; I will not forget Your word."
>
> —Psalm 119:9-16

> "Put the tablets of the testimony that I give you into the ark."
>
> —Exodus 25:16

> "Without revelation people run wild, but one who keeps the law will be happy."
>
> —Proverbs 29:18

> "There is a way that seems right to a man, but its end is the way to death."
>
> —Proverbs 14:12

> "When a land is in rebellion, it has many rulers, but with a discerning and knowledgeable person, it endures."
>
> —Proverbs 28:2

> "Disaster pursues sinners, but good rewards the righteous."
>
> —Proverbs 13:21

2. Saint Francis of Assisi said, "Preach always. And if necessary, use words." What do you think he meant by that statement?

3. In the space below, write down each significant "area" of your life (school, family, work, sports, church, friendships, etc.), and record one way you can have a good testimony in each of those areas:

4. Look up the word "responsibility" in the dictionary, and write the definition below. Think of a prominent leader, and write down at least five major responsibilities that person takes in serving their followers.

5. Read the following Scripture passages in preparation for the next session: Proverbs 29:18, Proverbs 14:12, Proverbs 28:2, Proverbs 13:21.

## CHAPTER TWO

# Seeing the Big Picture

KEY QUOTE:
**If you can articulate a clear vision and demonstrate
that you have a workable plan to reach it, people will follow.
—Jeff Myers**

## CHAPTER AT A GLANCE

- Why we need vision.
- Acceptintg a vision that leads to success.
- The four stages of vision.
- The death of a vision.
- Whose vision is it anyway?

## Why We Need Vision

OF THE FOUR SECRETS of world-changing leaders, strategic vision is hardest to grasp. Sometimes it seems that you either have a vision or you don't. In fact, many people believe there are some of us who are simply "born visionaries," and the rest of us just follow along. In the video, though, we defined strategic vision as "Seeing the world as God sees it," and that way of thinking has magnificent implications for how we approach our need to establish a vision.

> "You never conquer a mountain. Mountains can't be conquered; you conquer yourself—your hopes, your fears."
>
> —Jim Whitaker
> (first American to reach the summit of Mount Everest)

The main point about strategic vision is that it is not *my* vision I want to take hold of but *God's*. It has to do with *His* plan for the world as revealed in Scripture, not my plan.

This does not mean that our "secular" plans are somehow inferior—for example, that getting a vision for building a business is any less a part of God's plan than building a church. It means that the distinction between *secular* and *sacred* is a false distinction. As Christians, *everything* we do—whether going on a mission trip or painting the bathroom—is to be done to God's glory.

Admittedly, this can be a very confusing point. One of my students at Bryan College, in a moment of exasperation, said, "Maybe I've misunderstood, but how can my running on Bryan's cross county team bring God just as much glory as someone leading another to saving faith in Jesus Christ?"

My reply was: "It's not about what brings the greater glory. Scripture says that whatever we do, we do it as unto the Lord. The goal of everything in the Christian's life is to reflect God's glory. It's not our place to set up the 'rankings' of what brings Him more glory. There are greater and lesser gifts mentioned in Scripture, but it is safe to say that leading someone to saving faith in Jesus Christ brings glory to God, and running cross country, when done to reflect God's glory, brings glory to Him as well."

This student's involvement on the cross country team seems to hinge on whether or not he feels it is a proper placement of his priorities. But God's vision transcends all of our thoughts about what comes first, what comes second, etc. In fact, there are two things about God's vision that tend to confuse us mere mortals.

### 1. God's Vision Is Bigger than I Am.

Each summer I speak to several hundred young, potential leaders through a program called Summit Ministries. I take great pains to point out to these students that they will experience the highest expression of their gifts—and ultimately that which brings true meaning and fulfillment—when they live in the service of a vision greater than themselves.

God rarely inspires us to a vision that we feel we can actually accomplish. Rather, he gives us a vision that seeks His glory, that requires us to be dependent on others, and that can only be accomplished in His strength. We need other people's gifts. If you've reached the point where you realize your need for others, a sense of vision is probably driving you. You know where you want to go, and you know you can't get there by yourself. Take Moses, for example. When God told him to tell Pharaoh, "Let my people go," it was an absurdly large task. Moses knew he wasn't up to it, and he told God as much. But God responded, in essence, "Who's the One that created you? Go, and I will give you the words to say."

### 2. God's Vision Doesn't Center on Me.

Those who think they are the center of their own reality fail to consider themselves in relationship to anything else. Their identity is shifting, malleable, and transitory. They don't know who they are, so they don't know where they are or where they *should be* going.

David Thompson, the great 18th century Canadian explorer, found that the natives never understood his attempts at map-making because of their narrow focus:

> Both Canadians and Indians often inquired of me why I observed the Sun, and sometimes the Moon, in the day time, and passed whole nights with my instruments looking at the Moon and Stars. I told them it was to determine the distance and direction from the place I observed to other places; neither the Canadians nor the Indians believed me for both argued that if what I said was the truth, I ought to look to the ground, and over it; and not the Stars.[1]

We need a fixed point of reference that lies outside of ourselves in order to achieve great things. A vision draws our eyes upward to something larger than ourselves, to a compelling ideal toward which we must press.

## Accepting a Vision that Leads to Success

The passage I quoted in the video, Proverbs 29:18 ("Without revelation, people run wild, but one who keeps the law will be happy"), frankly makes me chafe a bit. In "the flesh," I don't want restraints. I want a vision that frees me from restraints, not one that places more restraints on me. But a clear vision enables me to accept "restraints" because I see how they are essential to my success. Here are some examples from different situations in life:

• Sports teams with a vision to win the championship will be more willing to abide by the rigorous demands of a coach's training schedule.

• A young couple desiring to purchase a home is more motivated to scrimp and save rather than spend money on short-term desires.

• Students in a school more willingly abide by the rules if they see why those rules are in place and how they benefit by having boundaries.

• People work harder on the job when they see the vision of achieving a sales target.

Why is this so? Because a vision enlarges people's view of the world, creating a picture of a desired state and compelling them to attempt great deeds for something bigger than self.

## The Four Stages of Vision

In the video I explained the four stages of vision and want to give you here a clearer idea of what to do at each stage.

### Stage One Vision: Notice the Problem

A vision-driven leader is like a building contractor. Where others see a vacant lot, the contractor envisions a completed building. Contractors are successful because they are not limited by what others see; they perceive a deeper meaning. There is a crucial difference between *seeing* and *perceiving*:

• Seeing—To get an impression using the sense of sight.

• Perceiving—To understand something using powers of the mind.

Most people look at the world around them but fail to see what is really important. The Bible says "…the way of the wicked is like the darkest gloom; they don't know what makes them stumble" (Proverbs 4:19). Christians, on the other hand, should learn to see the world by the light of God's Word, the Bible. King David wrote, "Your word is a lamp for my feet and a light on my path" (Psalm 119:105). We should see a richer world, full of meaning, because of our personal relationship with the One who made it.

Many years ago Russian scientists developed a surgical procedure to restore sight to people who had been blinded early in life by an eye disease. Researchers who subsequently studied these newly-sighted patients were astounded to discover that since the patients had never been able to see, they did not know how to interpret and understand what they were looking at.

In one study, researchers blindfolded patients and asked them to feel the shape and texture of an apple and then an orange. Then the researchers removed the blindfolds and asked the patients to distinguish the difference

> "Champions know that success is inevitable; that there is no such thing as failure, only feedback."
>
> —Michael J. Gelb

> "You can have billiant ideas, but if you can't get them across, your ideas won't get you anywhere."
>
> —Lee Iacocca

between the apple and orange by sight. They found that it was impossible for the newly-sighted patients to do so. The patients could sense the difference in texture and shape, but those differences had no meaning without the experience of knowing what those textures and shapes *look like*.

In the same way, it is possible for Christians to see what is going on in the world without understanding what it means to them or to their faith. To have vision, Christians must combine the physical capacity of sight with the mental capacity of understanding and to be light bearers who help illuminate truth for others.

### Stage Two Vision: Sense the Urgency

When I was little, one of my favorite Sunday school songs was "This Little Light of Mine": "Don't let Satan blow it out (*pffff*). I'm gonna let it shine." The song comes from Matthew 5:14, where Jesus tells His disciples, "You are the light of the world."

When Jesus said this, it must have been a shocker. "Light of the world" was a title—a description if you will—given to people with great wisdom, such as eminent rabbis. By using it in reference to His disciples, Jesus showed that His truth is from God, and that it is to be communicated to the world through His disciples, despite their feelings of inadequacy.

Jesus' statement also had an urgency to it. As John MacArthur points out, "[T]he pronoun 'you' is emphatic. The idea is…'You are the only light of the world.' The world's corruption will not be retarded and its darkness will not be illumined unless God's people are its salt and light."[2] Jesus intended his disciples—then and now—to be light-bearers, bringing understanding and wisdom to the darkened human heart.

Darkness is powerless over light. The smallest light causes darkness to flee, and the greatest darkness cannot extinguish even the weakest light source. Amazing, isn't it? No matter how thick the darkness, a light will shine bright in the midst of it!

But if the light of Christ has such a magnificent effect, why is the darkness growing? Why, for example, do great revivals die out, great churches wane, Christian civilizations collapse, and Christian leaders fall? Why does darkness so often prevail?

In the early 1800s French sociologist Alexis deTocqueville studied America and wrote his observations in an enduring book, *Democracy in America*. In one particularly prophetic passage, he notes that many dynamic civilizations collapse through apathy and indifference rather than through invasion. "Some cultures may let the torch be snatched from their hands," deTocqueville said, "but others stamp it out themselves."[3]

I wonder if that's the explanation: we "lights" have become very good at extinguishing ourselves. We've all seen it: nations, communities and organizations that had a good thing going, but for whatever reason—complacency, moral failure, etc.— threw it all away. This tragedy happens to individuals, too.

Vision is important. You want people to follow you, not because you're in the business of collecting followers, but because you're moving purposefully toward a significant goal and you want—*need!*—others to walk with you. If you can articulate a clear vision and demonstrate that you have a workable plan to reach it, people will follow, you will have influence, and you will make a difference.

### Stage Three Vision: Anticipate Involvement

"Well, Dr. Jeff," you may be saying, "I like this idea of having a vision. I believe I'm one of the committed few. I can see that people will be looking to me for answers. But I don't have a compelling vision toward which to lead them!"

May I suggest several spiritual disciplines that many have found powerful in clarifying and shaping a vision?

*1. Pray for more faith.* God is faithful, but I am not. I find that I am regularly praying for more faith so that I can understand. I am like the man whose child Jesus healed from demon possession: "Immediately the father of the boy cried out, 'I do believe! Help my unbelief.'" (Mark 9:24).

Sometimes answers just don't come to us this side of eternity. I'll never forget singer/ songwriter Michael Card's comments when he spoke at the Summit at Bryan College a number of years ago: "Many people go to their graves with their most pressing questions unanswered."

And still, you and I must pray with David:

Why am I so depressed?
Why this turmoil within me?
Put your hope in God, for I will still
    praise Him,
        my Savior and my God.
        (Psalm 42:5)

*2. Build into others' lives.* I can't imagine how devastating it was to the Apostle Paul to be placed in prison during his prime ministry years. Yet it is clear from his letters that he never stopped teaching, discipling, and mentoring.

For example, shortly before his unjust death, Paul exhorted his protégé Timothy to persevere:

You therefore, my child, be strong in the grace that is in Christ Jesus. And what you have heard from me in the presence of many witnesses, commit to faithful men who will be able to teach others also. Share in suffering as a good soldier of Christ Jesus. (2 Timothy 2:1-3)

*3. Be in fellowship with God's anointed.* At Mt. Carmel Elijah presided over the total defeat of the prophets of Baal. God was victorious in front of the whole nation, and the thirsty land was quenched with rain. Then, filled with spiritual energy, Elijah outran Ahab's chariot!

Yet Elijah soon went from an extreme high to an extreme low. God supernaturally provided him with rest and sustenance and then reminded him that he was not alone: "But I will leave 7,000 in Israel—every knee that has not bowed to Baal and every mouth that has not kissed him" (1 Kings 19:18).

Elijah needed other believers so that he could maintain his vision. So do we.

## Stage Four Vision: Commit to Action

Despite the extreme importance of vision, we seem to have encountered a cultural crisis in the last few years in which people find it difficult—if not impossible—to grasp a vision for what God is doing in the world and how to be part of it. And Satan knows how to take full advantage of this lack of vision.

During the key identity-shaping years when the "light is coming on" for Christian young people, Satan launches his most devastating attacks. By the time these potential leaders are actually in the world, they're not shedding any light at all.

I don't know about you, but this pattern happened to me, starting in the fourth grade. By ninth grade, I hit the "off switch." After that, I was simply mustering the courage to go against my parents' convictions.

Thankfully, God intervened, showing me that my identity was in Him, not in what I could or could not do. Looking back, though, and through interviews and study, I'm starting to believe that somewhere between the ages of nine and eleven children decide either to become "influencers" or to become "influenced." Influencers are more likely to lead, and the influenced are likely to succumb to peer pressure.

How does this happen? How is it that our little "lights of the world" lose their shine just when the culture needs them the most? I once illustrated a possible scenario by lighting a lamp and explaining how marvelous it is that God has called us to be the light of the world. Then

"The quality of a man's life is in direct proportion to his commitment to excellence."

—Vince Lombardi
Legendary NFL football coach

> "Our plans miscarry because they have no aim. When a man does not know what harbor he is making for, no wind is the right wind."
>
> —Seneca

I explained that other people, sometimes carelessly, sometimes maliciously, "curse" rather than "bless."

As I spoke, I covered the lamp with poster board signs containing "curses" such as:

- "Who do you think you are?"
- "You can't do that!"
- "You're a loser."
- "You just don't have the potential."

After a very few minutes, the lamp was completely covered and the light barely visible.

Harmful past experiences, poor choices, harsh words, painful losses—all of these are curses that define our identity negatively and diminish our light source. And it's not just a problem that the culture sends these messages—we should expect that from a fallen world. No, the real problem is that we *believe the messages* rather than *believing God*, and we adjust our lives accordingly. We let the darkness convince us that our lights should be turned off.

It's as if we are saying, "I don't want to be God-defined. I choose to define myself. I don't want to obey God—I want to be a slave to the culture instead." But while we believe we are defining ourselves, the reality is that we are losing definition altogether. Suddenly, we face many choices without having any good way to make decisions. By pulling us away from God, the culture has committed identity theft on a grand scale: unsure of where we are, we have no sense of where to go, or how to get there.

My passion is to train wise leaders for the next generation. I'm convinced that as we understand our identity from *God's* perspective, as opposed to the culture's perspective, new vistas will open up to us—new ways of seeing God's worldview, new ways of seeing the mission He has prepared for us, new sources of inspiration for living life, new ways of having an eternal impact.

## The Death of a Vision

Some time ago at a conference I was reacquainted with a man I had not seen for several years. He shared his heart with me about a prolonged period of spiritual pain in his life. "I couldn't even read your newsletters—they were too painful," he explained. This anguished brother had left a profitable vocation to pursue full time Christian ministry only to see his vision implode right before his eyes. He wondered, "Did I somehow miss God's plan?"

Read through the lives of the great kingdom-advancing men and women in history, and it becomes clear that most experienced some sort of death of a vision. Sometimes it was for a short season, and these saints quickly regained their bearings and saw God's plan. Other times there was a lengthy season of uncertainty. Winston Churchill experienced this in the years leading up to World War II. One of his biographers, William Manchester, called it "his wilderness years."

I hesitate to "dissect" what happens in the death of a vision, because each circumstance is different. But in reading Scripture it seems that there are at least three situations in which God's people experience it.

*1. When God accomplishes His purposes differently than the way we imagined He would.* I don't know about you, but I regularly find myself "instructing" God on how we will work together... "Okay Lord, get in the huddle. Here's the play we're going to run..."

Scripture says God's ways are higher than our ways (Isaiah 55:9). As much as I think I can see, the reality is that my vision is limited by my mortality—I do not know what God's ultimate purposes in a situation really are. I see as though in a mirror, indistinctly (1 Corinthians 13:12).

Knowing that God's ways are higher—that He intends to accomplish infinitely more than I can imagine—can be frustrating, but it is ultimately comforting. Moses, for example, thought God would use him to bring *relief* to the Israelite slaves. Little did he know God would use him to bring *deliverance*. It took a long time in the wilderness before he was truly prepared for such an undertaking.

*2. When we miss the point and think we are central to the accomplishment of God's plan.* I must recognize that God may call me, but He does not *need* me to do what He is doing. Sometimes it takes a jolt of reality for me to humble myself in His presence. Jonah is a good example of this reality. After Jonah repented from running away from God's plan, he went to warn the city of Ninevah of its impending destruction. But God spared the people of the evil city because they repented. Apparently, because his warnings of destruction did not come true, this made Jonah feel foolish.

It is clear from Scripture that Jonah missed the point entirely. He even complained to God about God's mercy (see Jonah 4:1-2). Jonah had confused his message with the Lord's purpose. He saw himself as an indispensable part of God's work, and he missed the bigger picture of what God was doing.

*3. When God's primary goal is working on us.* I have had many seasons of ministry in which I thought God was working through me to accomplish something significant in the *world*, only to realize that God was working through the world to accomplish something signifi-cant in *me*. God is shaping you and me into the image of His Son, and nothing will stop Him. At the end of his time of trial, Job finally got it right when he said, "I know that You can do anything and no plan of Yours can be thwarted" (Job 42:2).

## Whose Vision Is It Anyway?

I love to think about vision. I love to talk about vision. I love to dream things up and to try to bring them into reality. But in the end, there is only one vision: God's. I succeed only when I gain insight into what God sees, sacrificing my own visions to the one vision which, in the end, is all that maters.

In this season of your life, you may not yet fully see the light, but you can still be light to others. Is your identity one of illumination? Are you willing to consider the possibility that God has chosen you to be a light bearer in this dark world? Find courage in St. Augustine's *Confessions*:

> But you, chosen generation, you weak things of the world, who have forsaken all, that ye may follow the Lord; go after Him, and confound the mighty; go after Him, ye beautiful feet, and shine ye in the firmament...He whom you cleave unto, is exalted, and hath exalted you. Run ye to and fro, and be known unto all nations.[4]

He who is exalted has exalted you. You are shining bright—reflecting His glory. Shine on!

> "The essence of leadership is a vision you articulate clearly and forcefully on every occasion. You can't blow an uncertain trumpet."
>
> —Theodore Hesburgh
> former president, University of Notre Dame

> "But Jonah was greatly displeased and became furious. He prayed to the Lord: 'Please, Lord, isn't this what I said while I was still in my own country? That's why I fled toward Tarshish in the first place. I knew that You are a merciful and compassionate God, slow to become angry, rich in faithful love, and One who relents from sending disaster."
>
> —Jonah 4:1-2

> "For now we see indistinctly, as in a mirror, but then face to face. Now I know in part, but then I will know fully, as I am fully known."
>
> —1 Corinthians 13:12

# Consider This

Take a few minutes, and jot down answers to these questions and statements. They will help you think through where you are in the process of grasping "the big picture."

● **Read 1 Samuel 16:1-13 aloud and think about the difference between God's view and Samuel's view of the man God had chosen to be king. What did Samuel seem to think made a good king? By contrast, what did God say? Is this lack of seeing the world from God's perspective a problem today? How so?**

● **Think of different goals some might pursue and how a person might be vision-driven in those pursuits.**

● **Recall the "Four Stages of Vision" chart in the video. The four steps are (1) noticing the problem, (2) sensing the urgency, (3) anticipating involvement, and (4) committing to action. Taking each stage in turn, think of people you know or have heard of who faithfully practice those steps, and in the space below write what you see in them.**

# Follow-Up Exercise

The Bible is full of examples of people who made a difference because they had a vision. In order to see the world from God's perspective, we can look at examples of men and women in Scripture. Look up and read each of the following passages. Write a summary of the verse and take time to think about and jot down answers to each of the questions.

1. *Notice* the Problem: 2 Kings 6:9-17

   • Why was Elisha not worried?

2. *Sense* the Urgency: Esther 3:1-4:17

   • What did Esther first do in response to the horrible news?

   • How did she demonstrate her concern when it came time for action?

3. *Anticipate* Involvement: Isaiah 6:1-8

   • What must Isaiah have believed in order to respond as he did?

   • How might Isaiah have responded if he didn't feel that he could take responsibility?

4. *Commit* to Action: Judges 4:1-16

   • Why did Deborah commit to action? Many people fail to have vision because they are afraid or because they are complacent about the need for action.

   • Look up "fear" in the dictionary and write the definition below:

"Now there are different gifts, but the same Spirit. There are different ministries, but the same Lord. And there are different activities, but the same God is active in everyone and everything. A manifestation of the Spirit is given to each person to produce what is beneficial."

—1 Corinthians 12:4-7

"A man's heart plans his way, but the Lord determines his steps."

—Proverbs 16:9

> "If you tell me how you get your feeling of importance, I'll tell you what you are. That determines your character. That is the most significant thing about you."
>
> —Dale Carnegie

> "For it was You who created my inward parts; You knit me together in my mother's womb. I will praise You, because I have been remarkably and wonderfully made. Your works are wonderful, and I know [this] very well."
>
> —Psalm 139:13-14

The list below includes things many Christians fear. On a scale of 1 to 5, circle how much you fear each one (1=not very much, 5=a lot).

| | |
|---|---|
| • Failing at something you really want to accomplish | 1 2 3 4 5 |
| • Uncertainty about how life will change if you succeed | 1 2 3 4 5 |
| • Starting a conversation with a stranger | 1 2 3 4 5 |
| • Gaining new knowledge | 1 2 3 4 5 |
| • Uneasiness about what the future holds | 1 2 3 4 5 |
| • Not knowing God's will for your life | 1 2 3 4 5 |
| • Public speaking | 1 2 3 4 5 |
| • Sharing your faith with your friends | 1 2 3 4 5 |
| • Standing up for someone who is being talked about behind his or her back | 1 2 3 4 5 |
| • Being rejected by your friends | 1 2 3 4 5 |
| • Other people not listening to your ideas | 1 2 3 4 5 |
| • Being physically harmed | 1 2 3 4 5 |
| • Losing someone close to you | 1 2 3 4 5 |
| • Making commitments | 1 2 3 4 5 |

• **Look up "complacency" in the dictionary and write the definition below:**

Check the reasons below which you think describe why people are so complacent.

____ Fear of what others will think
____ A feeling of being let down by God
____ Feeling that God is not listening
____ Confusion about right and wrong
____ A belief that Christianity isn't right for everyone
____ A feeling of not needing God
____ A desire to explore other religions
____ Apathy
____ Boredom
____ A desire to engage in sin
____ Anger at God
____ Anger at family members
____ Bad experience at church
____ Bad example of other Christians
____ Non-Christian friends
____ Non-Christian teachers
____ Feeling they can't make a difference

____ _____
____ _____
____ _____

 **Read the following Scripture passages in preparation for the next session: Psalm 139:13-14, 1 Corinthians 12:4-7, Proverbs 16:9.**

# Living Like a Winner

## CHAPTER AT A GLANCE

- Discovering your mission in life.
- Who are you anyway?
- You can't do anything you want to do.
- Where does identity *really* come from.
- R = Review.
- A = Anticipate.
- C = Consult.
- E = Enact.
- The end of the matter and the beginning of the matter.

## Discovering Your Mission in Life

As WE DISCUSSED IN CHAPTER TWO, people generally follow those who can articulate a compelling vision. A "mission" is a vision for what you want to do, along with a plan for how to do it. You can't buy it. No one can give it to you. Your mission emerges out of a combination of your God-given design and the circumstances of your life. Since no one else was made like you, and no one else's life is quite like yours, no one else can have your mission. It is yours alone, and it is your choice as to whether to fulfill it.

But this all begs one very important question, doesn't it? How can you discover your mission if you don't know who you are?

> "God wanted to make known to those among the Gentiles the glorious wealth of this mystery, which is Christ in you, the hope of glory."
>
> —Colossians 1:27

> "Do not covet your neighbor's wife, his male or female slave, his ox or donkey, or anything that belongs to your neighbor."
>
> —Exodus 20:17

> "Do nothing out of rivalry or conceit, but in humility consider others as more important than yourselves."
>
> —Philippians 2:3

## Who Are You Anyway?

"How do you know that you exist?" the professor asked, a sly grin on his face. It was eight o'clock in a Monday morning philosophy class. This was completely unfair! I looked around the room and realized that my classmates also were at a loss for words.

"Oh great," I thought. "If we can't even prove that we *exist*, what *can* we know for sure?"

This professor was tapping into the ultimate question of *identity*: what defines the meaning of your or my existence? And it's not just an academic question. If we know who we are and why we're here, then we can develop a sense of purpose and begin traveling down the path of eternal impact.

My college sociology professor told me that "who we are" is a combination of many factors, including spiritual upbringing, family history, culture, knowledge, worldview, and the environment. Perceptions also play a huge part, he said—people take on roles based on what they think others expect of them.

The philosphy professor I mentioned earlier never brought up the possibility that we are endowed by our Creator with a unique set of gifts and talents. Such an idea would have been laughed off as naive. To think that a person's identity would be permanent or enduring would have been considered absurd. The philosopher's brand of naturalistic thinking considers that unless evolution can account for something, it doesn't exist.

This didn't bother my classmates, at least not at first. It seemed the professor was saying we could become whatever we wanted to be—we were our own measuring stick of success! "You can do anything you want to do" has become the mantra of a generation. But is that the true picture?

## You Can't Do Anything You Want to Do

Although it may *sound* nice to say you can do anything you want to do, think of how damaging this philosophy is at root:

• *It is selfish*, emphasizing what we *want* rather than what we *ought to seek*. The right question is, "What *should* I do?" not "What do I *want*?" It is not you, but Christ in you that is the hope of glory (Colossians 1:27).

• *It is covetous*. When I seek satisfaction apart from God's purposes, I end up imitating others: "'So and so' looks successful, and I want to be like him or her." Or in a smug, inverse form of covetousness: "'So and so' is flawed—I'm glad I'm not like him or her." We are not to covet (Exodus 20:17), and we are to esteem others rather than look down on them (Philippians 2:3).

• *It is self-defeating*. How many people have been led to believe they can succeed at something if they want it badly enough, and they literally wreck their lives—and the lives of others—trying to do something God never intended them to do? We should remember that each person is part of the body. No one is designed to do everything (1 Corinthians 12:11-12).

• *It is schizophrenic*. When all is said and done, how do you really know what you want? Maybe what you think you want isn't what is best. And there's the real rub! What seems right to us may actually be wrong and dangerous (Proverbs 14:12).

Modern technology has made it even harder to discover our true identity. Cell phones, blogs, wireless Internet, and other technological innovations have convinced many that their identity is virtual—that it doesn't exist in time and space. But if your "life" is not actually located in physical space, then what happens when you become disconnected from your gadgets? Do you actually lose your identity?

The postmodern mindset has taken us to an ironic extreme of not-knowing self: Rather than living *virtuously* by seeking our God-given identity, we live *virtually* in a make-believe world, constructing whatever identity we think fits the occasion.

## Where Does Identity Really Come From?

To have an enduring sense of identity means that our sense of meaning, influence, and destiny is rooted in *who God designed us to be.* What God desires for us is so much greater than what we want for ourselves that if we reject God's design and try to construct our own identities, we always feel inadequate. C. S. Lewis wrote:

> We are half-hearted creatures, fooling about with drink and sex and ambition when infinite joy is offered us, like an ignorant child who wants to go on making mud pies in a slum because he cannot imagine what is meant by the offer of a holiday at the sea.[1]

So if identity is not about what we *want*, what *is* it about?

It's about God, who has gifted you with an inspiring design so that you may glorify Him. "Inspiration" means to "breathe into." Just as God breathed life into Adam, he has breathed a powerful, significant, unique gift into your life.

How do we know God has done this? First, because He made us. The psalmist writes in Psalm 139: 13-14: "For it was You who created my inward parts; You knit me together in my mother's womb. I will praise You, because I have been remarkably and wonderfully made."

The things you know how to do, what you're skillful at, what you cannot *not* do—all of these were given to you by a loving creator. Because of sin, however, we humans tend to either abuse or abandon our design. But that doesn't change the fact that God put it there or that He wants to be glorified by it.

We also know God is the key to our identities because He anointed us. When we trust Christ, our natural gifting takes on a new significance. As we grow, we learn that our design was not intended to lift *us* up, but to glorify *God*. Not that our gifts change, but when they are anointed by the Holy Spirit, they are restored to their original intent.

The New Testament word translated as *anointing* comes from the Greek word *chrisma*. A Christian, essentially, is one who has an anointing from the Holy Spirit (1 John 2:20). The work of the Spirit is manifested a little differently in each person by that person's unique gifts, as 1 Corinthians 12:4-7 notes:

> Now there are different gifts, but the same Spirit. There are different ministries, but the same Lord. And there are different activities, but the same God is active in everyone and everything. A manifestation of the Spirit is given to each person to produce what is beneficial.

We can know we have been gifted by God and that our gifts not only inspire purpose, joy, and fulfillment in ourselves, but in others as well.

In the video I used the R.A.C.E. (Review, Anticipate, Consult, Enact) formula to bring out important questions that can help you discern your God-given identity. Let's take some time now to review and expand on those points.

## R = Review

If God designed you, then your past experiences should give ample evidence of what happens when you live out your gifts. I experienced an enormous breakthrough when I first understood this. I reviewed my life and discovered that I find great joy in (1) strategically changing things, and (2) explaining complex ideas in simple, practical terms. I am always happiest and most productive when I can change things and teach.

> "But one and the same Spirit is active in all these, distributing to each one as He wills.
> For as the body is one and has many parts, and all the parts of that body, though many, are one body—so also is Christ."
>
> —1 Corinthians 12:11-12

> "There is a way that seems right to a man, but its end is the way to death."
>
> —Proverbs 14:12

> "But you have an anointing from the Holy One, and you all have knowledge."
>
> —1 John 2:20

Many people find it difficult or frustrating to review their life experiences because they have become accustomed to taking a few pieces of information about themselves and branding themselves with some unhelpful label—"I'm a 'people person'" or "I'm an introvert." In doing so, people are in danger of using these labels to pigeon-hole themselves—and one another. Perhaps these examples will ring a bell:

- If you're a "detail person," you have been encouraged to work with numbers or machines rather than people.

- If you're outgoing, you have been told you would be great in sales.

- If you're an "introvert," you have been steered away from sales. Or leadership. Or anything dealing with people.

- If you're good at working with your hands, you have been discouraged from pursuing a liberal arts education.

- If you're "college prep" material, you have been discouraged from learning practical, hands-on skills.

- If your IQ isn't in the stratosphere, you have been encouraged to settle into a cubicle and serve those higher on the food chain.

To live like a winner, you must get beyond this kind of thinking. You are not a mere animal that reacts to the world around you. You have a mind and soul, and you think and act intentionally (Hebrews 4:12). Labels will always be inadequate to describe who you truly are.

That's why personality and social style tests, while informative, can never reveal your deepest design. Instead of taking more tests, I encourage you to look at what you find interesting, how you enjoy working, and what makes you feel more alive.

Let me tell you how this worked for me. As a child, I was extremely shy and was told time and again that I could never speak publicly, teach, or influence others. One vocational sur-

vey even hinted that I should work "in nature" where I could be alone, but my social planners were dead wrong. I have since discovered that operating in my God-inspired giftedness I *can* speak, teach, and influence lots of people.

Admittedly, the insights I share here merely scratch the surface. I suggest you also get a copy of *Finding a Job You Can Love* by Ralph Mattson and Arthur F. Miller, Jr. or *48 Days to the Work You Love* by Dan Miller. These books lead you step-by-step to discover your design and make decisions based on what you find to be true about yourself. In the meantime, I've reviewed below three steps to finding the thread of your inspired gift.

## 1. Write down ten accomplishments which have given you a great sense of satisfaction.

We're not just talking about end results you experienced, but times when you enjoyed the process as well as the results. For example, "In fourth grade I sold more greeting cards than anyone else in a class fund-raiser. I gained satisfaction by surprising my classmates and teacher—they didn't think I had it in me."

Then, look over your list and brainstorm several "themes" that tie these accomplishments together. For instance, did you enjoy helping others? If so, helping them in what way? What about helping gave you joy?

Some time ago a student excitedly told me about his mission trip to a third world country helping people recover from a natural disaster. As a result, he thought he felt called to be a missionary.

I asked, "Is it possible that the term 'missionary' is too broad? It seems that your real source of joy came from comforting people in distress and giving them hope, not specifically being on the mission field."

He agreed, so instead of pursuing general missions work, he pursued a career with a mission agency which focuses on disaster relief. "Mission work" was too broad of a category to fully utilize his gifts or to give him the sense of fulfilling his call.

## 2. With what do you like to work?

This question helps build confidence in the specific skills God has given you. Some folks prefer working with concepts, others with details. Some work with people, other with ideas. Some work with plans, others with tools.

Reflect on your work to discern the answer to this question. Of course, everyone ends up doing work some of the time that they don't prefer, but if you know your ideal work arrangement you can set goals and spend more time in what you are best at.

## 3. What triggers you to action?

If you and I were assigned the same job, we would each do it for different reasons. Some of us act out of a sense of obligation, others because they enjoy solving problems, and still others because they receive a sense of accomplishment.

Some individuals look for opportunities to impress people. Others just want respect. Many folks like to "come to the rescue" in emergencies while others love succeeding against great odds.

I have found that knowing what triggers me to action helps me turn less-than-ideal situations into deeply satisfying ones. For example, as a college student I spent a summer remodeling warehouses for my grandfather. It was dirty, hard work in extremely hot (miserable!) conditions.

The work itself didn't take much brain power, so I used my mind to imagine all of the businesses I could start that would utilize that warehouse space. I brainstormed how they would operate and imagined accomplishing something great.

This did not improve my work conditions, but it did make them more bearable. It doesn't matter to me that none of those business ideas ever materialized. Through the mental exercise,

I learned how to develop a spirit of creativity and innovation.

Invest some time this week brainstorming accomplishments that gave you satisfaction, paying attention to what you like to work with, and contemplating what triggers you to action. These steps will help you see your surroundings differently—as an opportunity for creativity. As you understand yourself better, you will find yourself intentionally moving toward the kind of work and life God meant for you to have.

## A = Anticipate

To "anticipate" your mission means to gain specific insight into how you are wired by what happens to you and around you. "Anticipate" yourself by considering these questions:

- Why did God choose to have you born when He did?

- Why did God place you in the family, school, town and nation He did?

- What opportunities or challenges have you been given by God?

Many people have discovered their gifts by tuning in to the lessons God wanted them to take away from their life experiences.

To anticipate what God wants you to learn from your experiences, you must have faith in God's providence. Providence comes from two words: "pro," meaning "before," and "noseo," "to think." Hence, "providence" means "to think ahead"—forethought. God provided for you by the design He built into you. God supplies all of your needs (Philippians 4:19), instructing and teaching the way you should go (Psalm 32:8).

It takes faith and patience to learn to see the world from God's perspective. Many people give up and embrace other worldviews. Here are some of the more popular, deceptive such views:

> "For the word of God is living and effective and sharper than any two-edged sword, penetrating as far as to divide soul, spirit, joints, and marrow; it is a judge of the ideas and thoughts of the heart."
>
> —Hebrews 4:12

> "I studied the lives of great men and famous women, and I found that the men and women who got to the top were those who did the jobs they had in hand, with everything they had of energy and enthusiasm."
>
> —President Harry Truman

• Deism—The belief that God created the universe, wound it up like a clock, and is off on vacation while it winds down.

• Fatalism—The idea that unseen forces of nature have determined what will happen to us, both good and bad.

• Chance—The notion that everything in the universe came about by random processes and that human beings are insignificant creatures in a vast universe.

What would it look like to take a "providential" view of your life? Try it by using the three step process explained below.

### STEP 1: Look back.

Where did you come from? What experiences have shaped you into what you are today? Who has had a positive impact on you? What mistakes did you make that you want to be sure not to repeat?

As I've looked back over my life, I can discern how God either brought me through or allowed me to go through significant, shaping experiences. I believe God often wants me to learn from those experiences, to be humbly grateful for the good things and to trust His guidance in the bad things.

I suggest that you write down your personal findings in a journal. You might discover that your past experiences shape your future direction.

### STEP 2: Look around.

In his best-selling book *Experiencing God*, Henry Blackaby encourages people to find out what God is doing and go wherever that happens to be. What are some needs that you observe (in your family, work, church or community) to which you can positively contribute?

Ask God to bring to your attention what He wants you to be involved with. Make a list, pray about the possibilities, seek wise counsel, and act on what you discern.

### STEP 3: Look ahead.

If you had all the time or money in the world, what would you do? If you had one chance to make a difference, what would you do?

Spend some time studying the culture around you. Read about trends in society to see what kinds of opportunities and challenges lie ahead. What could you do to meet them?

Simon Peter, one of Jesus' disciples, is a good case study of God's providence. Few people in the New Testament were as bull-headed and clumsy as Peter. He was uncouth, unlearned and unaware of how God wanted to use him. Yet after denying Christ and being restored, Peter became an evangelist and endured tremendous persecution for his faith.

Toward the end of his life, Peter encouraged followers to actively seek their call by interacting with the world around them. He called Christians to "make every effort" to gain goodness, knowledge, self-control, perseverance, godliness, and brotherly kindness.

By doing this, Peter concluded, a person keeps from being ineffective and unproductive and also becomes more certain of his or her calling (2 Peter 1:5-11).

Because God cares for you and guides you, your everyday experiences, your past, and your opportunities serve as "markers" on your path. But you must actively seek them out and act on what you discover.

There is much uncertainty in our nation right now which means there may be difficult days ahead. But whatever happens, God, in His providence, will care for you and teach you through it all.

## C = Consult

To "consult" means to find those who are doing something interesting to you and to inquire about it. Ask questions, study, and brainstorm. To master a sport, you put yourself under the authority of a coach. To find success and meaning in life, you need a coach, too.

Author and pastor Gregg Harris notes that when the Queen of Sheba found out King Solomon was the wisest man who had ever lived, she responded by traveling to "test him with hard questions" (1 Kings 10:1). You probably know several Solomons. They may not be the wisest people who have ever lived, but you could learn a lot from them.

It occurred to me some time ago that the wisest people I know all have something in common: They voraciously seek wisdom! I know that sounds obvious, but it isn't. It takes humility to seek out the advice and input of others, and it is a constant struggle for me to overcome my pride and self-sufficiency in this matter.

But counsel from the right people is critical. Here are some questions to help you identify who they are:

- Who knows what you need to know?

- Who is doing what you would like to do?

- Who has credibility with others and is experiencing favor with God and man?

- Who will give you honest, constructive feedback?

- Who can encourage you and guide you?

Once you identify these folks, figure out how to learn from them. Read their books. Spend time observing them. E-mail or call them. Take them to lunch and ask questions.

What is stopping you from doing it? As my father always used to say, "If you ask, the answer is sometimes 'no.' If you don't ask, the answer is *always* 'no.'"

There is wisdom in a multitude of counselors (Proverbs 15:22). Here are six categories of Solomons you need to start interacting with right away:

*1. Trusted Friends and Relatives.* Don't neglect the obvious. Ask family members: "When you observe my life, what do you see

as my strengths and weaknesses?" If you are a student, ask your teachers: "Based on what you know about me, what do you think I would be good at?" Ask co-workers or your boss: "I want to take my work to the next level. What are some areas of strength or weakness that you think I could work on?"

*2. Spiritual Advisors.* Ask your pastor: "What kind of character qualities do you see in my life?" "How can I be stronger?" "How can I discover what is important to God about my life?"

*3. Mentors.* Think of the wisest people you know, and arrange to spend time with them. Prepare well for these meetings. Write out questions you would like to have answers to. Tell them that you admire them and want to learn from them. Ask if it is possible to take them to lunch or arrange to spend time together.

*4. Coaches.* If you want to know how to play a sport, you find a coach. If you want to explore an occupation or find out how to be wise and successful, you should do the same thing. I actually had a "business coach" who helped me build a Web site, improve my speaking, and develop products.

*5. Authorities.* Though you might not get to spend much time personally with well-known authorities, you can read their books, browse their Web sites, and subscribe to their publications. Years ago, as I struggled to develop a career in public speaking, I read *Speak and Grow Rich* by Lilly and Dottie Walters. Though the title sounds crass, this mother/daughter team gives tremendous advice on jump-starting a public speaking career, maintaining integrity, and serving clients well. I've never met these two women, but I have learned a great deal from them nonetheless.

*6. Heroes.* Perhaps there are people from the past (or who are still living) whom you admire greatly. Inspire yourself by reading biographies and autobiographies to discover what made them tick. Winston Churchill is one such

"And my God will supply all your needs according to His riches in glory in Christ Jesus."

—Philippians 4:19

"I will instruct you and show you the way to go; with My eye on you, I will give counsel."

—Psalm 32:8

> "...make every effort to supplement your faith with goodness, goodness with knowledge, knowledge with self-control, self-control with endurance, endurance with godliness, godliness with brotherly affection, and brotherly affection with love. For if these qualities are yours and are increasing, they will keep you from being useless or unfruitful in the knowledge of our Lord Jesus Christ. The person who lacks these things is blind and shortsighted, and has forgotten the cleansing from his past sins. Therefore, brothers, make every effort to confirm your calling and election, because if you do these things you will never stumble. For in this way, entry into the eternal kingdom of our Lord and Savior Jesus Christ will be richly supplied to you."
>
> —2 Peter 1:5-11

person for me. I've gained courage in the face of difficulties by following his example.

Start seeking out the Solomons in your life today. Make it a priority. As you do, your inspirational gift will spark to life, and you'll find a much greater sense of direction and purpose in life.

## E = Enact

To "enact" your mission means God will guide and steer you as you do what you think is best according to God's Word, your conscience, the guidance of the Holy Spirit, and the counsel of wise people.

Wise leaders decide what to do, and then they just do it. They still make mistakes, but they prefer to mess up while trying something than to succeed at doing nothing! In the end, success goes to those who start doing what they think is best.

Sadly, many people are unsure of what direction they should go so they just stop moving altogether. Can you honestly expect God to steer you if you are not going anywhere? Is it possible to steer a non-moving object? Obviously not.

The more engaged you are in living out what you know to be true, the more you'll learn and grow. A Department of Education study many years ago revealed that learners remember:

- 10% of what they read
- 20% of what they hear
- 30% of what they see
- 50% of what they see and hear
- 70% of what they say
- 90% of what they say and do

The very best way to learn something is to talk about it and act on it. Even if your activities don't relate directly to your inspired gift, you can learn a great deal and gain new skills by trying different activities and challenges.

Here are some questions to get you moving:

1. What things have you always wanted to try? What is stopping you?

2. If you could take just one hour a week to advance toward a goal, what would you do during that hour? What is stopping you?

3. If you do not have a clear sense of direction, what are five things you can do while you are waiting? What is stopping you?

4. What are the top three reasons you are not acting on your vision? What are three things you can do about each of those reasons?

Certainly, there are times where God says, "Be still" (Psalm 46:10), but this is usually when we are worn out from aggressive action. Be sure to get enough rest, but don't let fear or uncertainty prevent you from learning valuable lessons God has for you through everyday experiences!

## The End of the Matter, and the Beginning of the Matter

God has gifted us each with a multitude of gifts. As you discover and tap into your gifts, you will find a wealth of energy that will enable you to live a life full of meaning, influence, and joy.

It doesn't mean life will be easy. The sorrows of the fallen human condition surround us at all times. But knowing your gifts allows you to run like a champion in the race set out for you, knowing God will redeem your feeble efforts to serve His grand purposes. And this, in the end, is what makes life worth living. Press on!

# Consider This

Take a few minutes, and jot down answers to these questions and statements. They will help you identify important truths about the way God designed you.

- Dr. Myers says you can discover your design by looking at what you "can't *not* do." Do you agree with that? Is it possible to abuse that knowledge by using your gifts in the wrong way? If so, how?

- It is often said there is a "generation gap" between teenagers and adults. Do you think that's true? If so, why do you think younger people don't want to seek counsel from older people?

"Plans fail when there is no counsel, but with many advisers they succeed. "

—Proverbs 15:22

"Stand tall. The difference between towering and cowering is totally a matter of inner posture. It's got nothing to do with height, it costs nothing and it's more fun."

—Malcolm Forbes

● Dr. Myers defined "providence" as the belief that "God cares for us and guides us." List some of the ways God provides for us every day.

● If you had all the time, money and resources you could possibly need in order to make a difference in the world, what would you do?

# Follow-Up Exercise

Answer each question in the grid below as honestly as you can.

**Have you ever felt that God doesn't care—that he's not involved?**
_____ **Yes** _____ **No**

**Have you ever felt that no matter what you do, it won't make any difference?**
_____ **Yes** _____ **No**

**Have you ever felt that God is not in control, that everything is determined by chance?**
_____ **Yes** _____ **No**

**Have you ever been uncertain about what God wants you to do with your life?**
_____ **Yes** _____ **No**

**Have you ever wondered what God's will is for you?**
_____ **Yes** _____ **No**

**Have you ever worried about what the future holds?**
_____ **Yes** _____ **No**

**Have you ever wondered whether you are making the right decisions—the ones God wants you to make?**
_____ **Yes** _____ **No**

> "Stop your fighting—and know that I am God; exalted among the nations, exalted on the earth."
>
> —Psalm 46:10

If you have doubts about God's will for your life, you're not alone. It has been said that the number one fear of youth today is that they will not discover the purposes of their lives.

**Read 2 Peter 1:3-10**

- **What has God given us for life and godliness?**

- **Why has He done this?**

- **What effort does God want us to make in response?**

- **What will this effort help us do?**

- **What should this make us eager to do?**

> "In Him we were also made His inheritance, predestined according to the purpose of the One who works out everything in agreement with the decision of His will, so that we who had already put our hope in the Messiah might bring praise to His glory."
>
> —Ephesians 1:11-12

God has created every person to be unique, giving them a wide variety of talents and skills. Rate the following occupations on how spiritual they are as occupations for Christians (1=not at all spiritual, 5=highly spiritual).

| | |
|---|---|
| **Politician** | 1 2 3 4 5 |
| **Athlete** | 1 2 3 4 5 |
| **Missionary** | 1 2 3 4 5 |
| **Factory worker** | 1 2 3 4 5 |
| **Lawyer** | 1 2 3 4 5 |
| **Teacher** | 1 2 3 4 5 |
| **Pastor** | 1 2 3 4 5 |
| **Soldier** | 1 2 3 4 5 |
| **Engineer** | 1 2 3 4 5 |

God's people through the ages have taken part in every conceivable occupation. Heroes in the Bible were everything from shepherds to military leaders. According to Colossians 3:23-24, what is more important to God than the job you are in?

## PUTTING IT INTO PRACTICE

Look back at your notes for the "Living Like a Winner" video. Write a summary of each concept in the **R.A.C.E.** formula and answer the questions that follow.

### R = Review

One way of finding out what God has gifted you to do is to look back over your life and think of things you have accomplished which give you a great sense of satisfaction. For example, "When I was in fourth grade we sold greeting cards as a fund-raiser. I sold more sets of greeting cards than anyone else. I felt a great sense of satisfaction from this because it was the first time I had ever out-performed my classmates on a project." *Describe five things you have accomplished that gave you a great sense of satisfaction:*

1.

2.

3.

4.

5.

## A = Anticipate

Answer the following questions, and try to discover a pattern for how God has worked in your life: Why did God choose to have you born when He did? Why did God place you in the family, school, town and nation that He did? Based on the opportunities and challenges God has given you, what can you conclude about how God has shaped you?

## C = Consult

If you want to know about how to play a sport, you find someone to coach you. Similarly, if you want to explore an occupation or find out how to be wise and successful, you must find someone to learn from. Don't neglect the obvious people in your life who could give guidance. Ask your *parents*: "When you observe my life, what do you see as my strengths and weaknesses?" Ask your *teachers*: "Based on what you know about me, what do you think I would be good at?" Ask your *pastor*: "What kind of character qualities do you see in my life? How can I be stronger?

*What are some things you would like to learn, and who could teach you?*

"The queen of Sheba heard about Solomon's fame connected with the name of the Lord and came to test him with difficult questions. She came to Jerusalem with a very large retinue, with camels bearing spices, gold in great abundance, and precious stones. She came to Solomon and spoke to him about everything that was on her mind. So Solomon answered all her questions; nothing was too difficult for the king to explain to her. When the queen of Sheba observed all of Solomon's wisdom, the palace he had built, the food at his table, his servants' residence, his attendants' service and their attire, his cupbearers, and the burnt offierngs he offered at the Lord's temple, it took her breath away."

—1 Kings 10:1-5

"Whatever you do, do it enthusiastically, as something done for the Lord and not for men, knowing that you will receive the reward of an inheritance from the Lord—you serve the Lord Christ."

—Colossians 3:23-24

> "But who are you—anyone who talks back to God? Will what is formed say to the one who formed it, 'Why did you make me like this?' Or has the potter no right over His clay, to make from the same lump one piece of pottery for honor and another for dishonor? And what if God, desiring to display His wrath and to make His power known, endured with much patience objects of wrath ready for destruction? And [what if] He did this to make known the riches of His glory on objects of mercy that He prepared beforehand for glory—on us whom He also called, not only from the Jews but also from the Gentiles?"
>
> —Romans 9:20-24

## E = Enact

God will guide and steer you as you do what you think is best according to God's Word, your conscience, the guidance of the Holy Spirit, and the counsel of wise people. Wise leaders are successful because they decide what to do and then do it. They still make mistakes, but they would rather mess up while trying something than to succeed at doing nothing! According to Ephesians 6:13-18, what are the main actions God wants every Christian to take?

Read the following Scripture passages in preparation for the next session: Ephesians 1:11-12, 1 Kings 10:1-5, Ephesians 6:13-18, Deuteronomy 31:6, and Romans 9:20-24

## CHAPTER FOUR

# Leadership Fitness

KEY QUOTE:
**Leadership fitness is about learning to live well—
not fast, not slow, but well. It means learning to live a
balanced life as a reflex.**
**—Jeff Myers**

## CHAPTER AT A GLANCE

- It's a rat race out there
- Your view of motivation depends on your view of the world.
- Is what you're living for worth dying for?
- Taking on what you are designed to do.
- Marching to the drumbeat of God.
- Setting a reasonable pace.
- Taking time for recreation.
- The beginning begins now.

## It's a Rat Race Out There

EVERY YEAR I ASSIGN MY STUDENTS at Bryan College to read *Overload Syndrome* by Dr. Richard Swensen. They love it and hate it because Dr. Swensen's simple message is so convicting: we're trying to do too much. We're living longer, earning more money, experiencing more cultural opportunities and reaping more benefits from technological advancement than ever before. But when did the fun go out of life? Why are we more stressed, more tired and less fulfilled?

The world's response to this problem is to push harder. On television, through books, and on the radio, we get the messages: "Other people are doing more, why can't you? Others are succeeding, why are you being left behind?" None of us wants to be viewed as irresponsible or unsuccessful, so we search for ever new and potent experiences, concoctions, strategies, and techniques to boost our energy and keep us in the game.

Worse, there is no graceful way to bow out. Every once in awhile the news will report someone as having resigned from a high-stress position "to spend more time with their family." It sounds like a noble thing to do, but in the high-flying world of business and politics, "spending more time with family" is code for "caved in under the pressure," "wimped out," or even "got fired." Is there any way out of this rat race?

## Your View of Motivation Depends on Your View of the World

Judging solely by the people featured on magazine covers and fawned over on television, it's easy to conclude that pushing harder and working longer are normal activities. In reality, however, this "go for the gusto" attitude grows out of a naturalistic worldview that says "nature is all there is." What you see is what you get. When your earthly life is over, it's over. So work as hard as you can *now*. Get all you can *now*.

The biblical worldview, on the other hand, states that this life is preparation for the next. By living redemptively we are being restored to both our created design and our Creator. The habits, attitudes, and character we develop on this earth feed our eternal souls and point the way for others. Death is not the end—it's merely a change of address, an unfolding of our true nature.

If this is so, then true motivation comes from the inside out, from what God designed you to be. It is not sucked from the external environment. Rather, it is injected into your being from your God-given reserves of giftedness. These reserves, properly nurtured, are inexhaustible.

This lesson on "Leadership Fitness" means discovering a source of motivation that prepares you to continue for the long haul, to have something worth living—and dying—for.

## Is What You're Living For Worth Dying For?

Telemachus was a monk who lived during the decline of the Roman Empire. Despite having dedicated himself to a simple life of prayer and study, Telemachus once felt led to take a pilgrimage to Rome. There he was shocked by the decadence of the people and appalled by the brutal custom of Romans celebrating war victories by watching gladiators (slaves, enemy captives, and paid performers) fight one another to the death. Thousands would gather in the Coliseum to watch the spectacle, working themselves into a frenzy at the sight of the fighting and bloodshed.

As Telemachus watched, the gladiators emerged and saluted the Emperor with, "Hail, Caesar, we who are about to die salute thee!" Then they began to fight, wound and kill each other. In desperation Telemachus leapt into the arena and tried to stop the fighting, shouting to the crowd: "Do not celebrate God's mercy for your victory by murdering each other!" In response to cries of "Down with him," the gladiators pounced on Telemachus, stabbing him to death.

But Telemachus did not die in vain. The hearts of even the most bloodthirsty were turned by seeing the gentle monk killed for trying to stop this cruel and evil custom. Legend has it that from that day forward, no gladiator fights were ever again held at the Coliseum.

What explains the motivation of a person like Telemachus, who was willing to sacrifice his own life to save the lives of people who seemingly didn't even want to be saved? I would submit that he didn't even think about it. He had cultivated godly character for so long time that doing the right thing was a *reflex* for him.

Leadership fitness is about learning to live *well*—not *fast*, not *slow*, but *well*. It means learning to live a balanced life *as a reflex*. When people live this way, they develop an emotional and physical reserve that makes it possible to ramp up to a high level, accomplish a significant goal, and then move back to a balanced state. What we're interested in here is situational motivation—how to be motivated when motivation is needed, rather than how to maintain a constant state of high energy.

Through observation and study, I've come to believe there are four things that people who are motivated in this way do to prepare themselves for action: they take on what they are designed to do, they march to the drumbeat of God, they set a reasonable pace, and they take time for recreation.

We learned about each of these points in the video, but let's supplement your understanding of each by discussing them in more detail.

## Taking on What You're Designed to Do

To do what you are designed to *do*, you must know what you are designed to *be*. If you're unclear about this, refresh your memory of the strategies in Chapter Three. You don't need to know *everything* about your design, but you should be prepared to act on what you do know. For example, you should discern how you like to work and the kinds of work that return energy to you and make you feel more alive.

Lots of people make it to this step. They know what they are designed to do, and they long to do it. Unfortunately, there are many barriers that stand in the way: lack of opportunity, people who don't understand, prior commitments, a busy schedule. Some folks just feel lucky to make it through each day, let alone to find joy, meaning, and satisfaction.

That's why it's vital for you to identify and knock down whatever barriers stand in your way. To get at those obstacles, ask yourself several questions.

*1. What is stopping me?* I'm of the personality type that likes to have a certain level of organization in order to operate. I'm writing this on a Monday morning after a busy week of travel. When I woke up, I set about unpacking my suitcase, putting things away, and straightening my desk. I didn't do any deep cleaning—just some surface things to make it easier for me to concentrate. Think about what needs to be "cleaned up" in your life in order for you to operate more effectively. Hebrews 12:1 says, "[L]et us lay aside every weight and the sin that so easily ensnares us, and run with endurance the race that lies before us."

*2. What needs to be done?* One of my friends, John, is a family pastor for a rapidly growing church. I asked him how busy-ness affects the people in his congregation. He said, "Often times our chaotic lifestyle propels us to be more interested in activity than accomplishment." That's important. A balanced life is not about my level of activity—whether or not I appear busy—but what I've actually gotten done. As 1 Corinthians 9: 26 instructs, "Therefore I do not run like one who runs aimlessly"—we should have a destination and a goal in mind.

*3. What one thing could I do over and above what I'm responsible for?* There are a lot of chores in life. I must work to support my family and take care of those I'm responsible for. My boss expects me to do what he has hired me to do. But what one thing could I do today that would go above and beyond? Could I, for example, take 30 minutes at the end of the day to read a book that would help renew my vision for living out my design?

*4. What is my attitude?* I once received a letter from Tammy, a subscriber to my newsletter, who said:

I can't help but think that my attitude towards all the things I do helps contribute to my energy level. I believe negative attitudes drain a person's energy levels quicker. So choosing to be content and claiming

> "People who smile tend to manage, teach and sell more effectively, and to raise happier children. There's far more information in a smile than a frown."
>
> —James McConnell

the joy of the Spirit in our life helps us to use the energy we do have more effectively. I believe the Lord is faithful at filling our cups once we've poured ourselves out for Him.

Tammy is absolutely right. Proverbs 17:22 explains, "A joyful heart is good medicine, but a broken spirit dries up the bones." A joyful spirit lifts you—and others—up. A negative or condemning spirit drives you—and others—into the ground.

## Marching to the Drumbeat of God

As I pointed out in the video, Jesus didn't always do what other people wanted Him to do, but He was always completely focused on what God wanted Him to do. This is a crucial point. We tend to live much of our lives in response to what others want, or what we *think* others want of us. The motivated person, however, seeks God *first*, asking questions like:

- What is God concerned about?
- What is most important?
- What short-term need is actually trying to short-circuit long-term success?

Jesus said, "[S]eek first the kingdom of God and His righteousness, and all these things will be provided for you" (Matthew 6:33).

I try to squeeze a few days of writing into my schedule each month. My team members, Corey and Cynthia, and my wife and children, make sacrifices so I can take this time. Yet when each writing day approaches, I feel tempted to waste it. This morning, for instance, I downloaded my e-mail and spent almost two hours responding to messages. But this chapter needed to be written *today* while every one of those messages could have waited. What I should have done was to intentionally *procrastinate on things that need to be put off*, and exercise the discipline *to do today what can only be done today.* As you see, I'm still learning!

Over the years, though, I have found several ways to maintain focus on what's most important. Hopefully, you'll adopt these good habits sooner than I did, and therefore reap the benefits earlier in life.

One crucial point is to operate within God-defined seasons. God created time, and that is a profound thing when you consider the implications. God is an eternal being who is not bound by time, yet He operates within time. He organized nature into repeating periods of time—days and seasons.

Here are two ways to cooperate with the seasons of time God established in nature:

*1. The 24-hour day.* No matter how bad today is, tomorrow morning I have the opportunity to begin anew. Scripture says, "Because of the Lord's faithful love we do not perish, for His mercies never end. They are new every morning; great is Your faithfulness!" (Lamentations 3:22-23).

Here's how I make the most of the renewal of each day: every morning I jot down just one achievable goal. I don't try to conquer the world—one goal is enough to focus my action throughout the day. I keep my goals organized in a personal digital assistant (PDA). Others use a white board or index cards. The method you choose doesn't matter as much as writing your goal down in a place that is easy to see during the day.

I also decide in advance how much time I will dedicate to each project on which I'm planning to work. I have learned, for example, that an article that takes four hours to write usually is not substantially better than an article that takes three hours to write. And if I really focus my time and attention, I can accomplish that same amount of work in two hours.

If you're writing a report, decide how much time you will invest, say 30 minutes. Then plan the 30 minutes: 5 minutes to outline each main point, 10 minutes to collect information, 10 minutes to write, and 5 minutes to edit and print. The goal is not a perfect report, but the best report you can write in 30 minutes!

Invariably, a report that takes one-hour to produce isn't much better than one that takes 30 minutes. So planning allows you to focus your energy and accomplish more in less time.

*2. The season.* I do not believe it is God's will for you to pile activities on top of activities on top of more activities. "There is an occasion for everything, and a time for every activity under heaven," says Ecclesiastes 3:1. Rather than overwhelming yourself, try sequencing your activities by defining a "sunset" for each thing you do. If there isn't a defined ending point, set one. Let's say you're asked to teach a Sunday school class. Tell the Sunday school coordinator: "I'll be happy to teach the class for one quarter (13 weeks)."

Once when my wife, Danielle, was asked to lead the single mom's group at our church, we prayed about it and decided it was not wise to permanently add this activity to our already busy schedule. But we determined Danielle could host the weekly meetings in our home, just for the summer, in order to teach a curriculum on parenting skills. At the end of the summer, Danielle and the group celebrated what they had learned and called that season to a close. Please note well: This isn't an excuse to avoid committing to important things but simply a strategy to head off over-commitment.

In addition to operating in God-defined seasons, leading a balanced life entails focus on maintaining the spiritual disciplines that prepare you for spiritual victory. Some Christians see spiritual growth as a checklist: Did I read my Bible today? Did I express the joy of the Lord throughout the day?

Checklists can remind you to do the right thing. The problem with a checklist mentality, however, is that it can make you think of spiritual disciplines as something that needs to be done—like washing the dishes—instead of preparation for spiritual warfare.

Having said that, though, you'll find yourself more attuned to God's plan if you build time into each day for the practice of spiritual disciplines such as:

• *Bible reading.* Get to know God's plan for the world, and what has happened to people through time as they either obeyed or disobeyed God. God's Word gives us insight and direction. The psalmist wrote, "Your word is a lamp for my feet and a light on my path" (Psalm 119:105).

• *Prayer.* Praise God for his awesomeness, acknowledge your dependence on Him, and make your requests known. In fact, 1 Thessalonians 5:17 enjoins us to "Pray constantly."

• *Meditation.* Psalm 77:12 says, "I will reflect on all You have done and meditate on Your actions." Think deeply about God—who He reveals Himself to be in Scripture, and what His mission is for the world.

## Setting a Reasonable Pace

In a major land-clearing effort at our house some years ago, my chain saw became so dull that logs which ordinarily took 10 minutes to cut were now taking 20 or 30 minutes. The remedy? I invested 15 minutes sharpening the saw and was once again able to finish the work in the appropriate amount of time.

Gregg Harris, a pastor and seminar leader, once told my leadership class: "If you're operating in God's will, a reasonable amount of work each day will be sufficient. If you're not operating in God's will, no amount of work will be sufficient."

For most people, the amount of work is not the issue, but their stamina is. You've only got one body, and it's important to take care of it. A wise leader does not sacrifice his or her body's basic needs to accomplish a task. That's like increasing your speed as you drive by a gas station on an empty tank. Without refilling the tank you *will* run out of gas, and whether you've made it five more miles or ten miles will make very little difference when you're stranded by the side of the road.

Here are some ideas for quickly boosting your energy:

*1. Drink lots of water.* I know this sounds simplistic, but many people swear by it. Some who believe this is important suggest drinking

> "Nothing will ever be attempted if all possible objections must first be overcome. Nothing will ever be perfect before you begin."
>
> —Samuel Johnson

"In religion as in war and everything else, comfort is the one thing you cannot get by looking for it. If you look for truth, you may find comfort in the end: If you look for comfort, you will not get either comfort or truth."

—C. S. Lewis

"Speech is a mirror of the soul: as a man speaks, so is he."

—Publius Syrus
(42 B.C.)

"So the heavens and the earth and everything in them were completed. By the seventh day, God completed His work that He had done, and He rested on the seventh day from all His work that He had done. God blessed the seventh day and declared it holy, for on it He rested from His work of creation."

—Genesis 2:1-3

several glasses—up to eight—a day. Much lack of energy, they say, is a result of dehydration.

*2. Nutrition.* Most nutritionists recommend unprocessed and low-fat whole foods and at least five servings of fruits and vegetables per day.

*3. Sleep.* Studies show that most adults need eight hours of sleep per night. A lack of sleep has a cumulative effect, leading to "sleep debt," a dangerous condition in which your body and mind lack creativity and are prone to error. Many times when I talk about sleep, my college students object: "Dr. Myers, the residence hall is loud. I would like to sleep, but I can't." To these students I suggest something that has always worked for me: ear plugs. When I stay in hotels I always put them in as I crawl into bed. They diminish the noise enough that it doesn't distract me from sleep. Packages of ear plugs are available for purchase in the sporting goods or hardware sections of many stores—for less than $2.00. It's the best money I've spent!

By the way, short naps can be helpful, but they don't replace nighttime sleep. A 10-20 minute nap, one that is long enough to take the edge off of your tiredness but not long enough to disrupt night-time sleep patterns, might be helpful. Years ago I learned of a technique to maximize "power naps." Lie down with your head and feet elevated, take a deep breath and hold it in while flexing your muscles. Exhale. Repeat this twice. Set an alarm for 15 minutes and close your eyes. I have found that I wake more energized than if I had slept for an hour!

By God's design, sleep is important. God is in charge of everything, and we don't need to deprive ourselves of sleep to accomplish His will. Psalm 127:2 points out, "In vain you get up early and stay up late…certainly He gives sleep to the one He loves."

*4. Exercise.* A friend of mine, Wayne, is a doctor. He says, "When I really need energy, I try to get some exercise (principle of sowing and reaping), when I give out energy, I get more back." Interestingly, exercise helps improve your sleep as well. A study by Stanford University found that people who exercise 30-40 minutes a day, four days a week, sleep better. After 16 weeks of study, "the exercise group on average slept nearly an hour longer per night, took less time to fall asleep, spent less time napping and reported an improvement in the overall quality of their nighttime sleep." The study also showed that those who exercised in the afternoon or before supper time slept better and avoided the afternoon doldrums.[1]

If you're keeping your body healthy and maintaining a healthy pace, you've got a great head start. But you still want to feel the inspiration, focus and energy that come from tackling your tasks with vigor. Scripture tells us to make the most of our time (Colossians 4:5), literally, to restore time to the power it had before sin made such a mess of the world. As part of their redeeming time, leaders must avoid junk food of the mind—most of what's on television, most magazines, and most radio programs.

Opportunities abound to fill your mind in productive ways. For instance, I spend as much of my commute time as possible listening to audio books. I buy them used on the Internet for half the original price and listen to them everywhere I go. I once calculated that if a person has a 20-minute commute to and from work and listens to audio books that entire time, he or she would take in the equivalent class time of *five* doctoral degrees by retirement age. You can't benefit from what you don't know, and there are a lot of good thinkers and writers out there whose work will inform and inspire you as a leader.

Am I saying that you shouldn't have any down time? No, certainly not. Sometimes being alone with your thoughts is a great investment of time. I carry a journal everywhere I go, and sometimes I just sit and observe, writing down what I see. The more I've tried to cultivate a life of contemplation, the more I've noticed there is noise everywhere. There isn't a store, airport, hotel, or restaurant that doesn't have television, radio, or music playing continually. If you want to get away from the noise, you have to be purposeful about it.

## Taking Time for Recreation

Earlier in this chapter we talked about cooperating with the seasons of nature God has built into creation. But there is one other cycle God invented that He did not build into creation. Rather, He used it as the basic *structure* of creation. It's the seven-day week. Think about it: days and seasons are naturally-occurring cycles, but the week exists only in the mind of God. On six days God created, and on the seventh day He rested. That's our pattern—six days of work and a seventh day to rest and enjoy God's presence.

The great secular humanist movements in history, such as the National Convention in revolutionary France, understood the power of the seven-day week to facilitate worship and God-honoring rest. Voltaire, the atheistic French Revolutionary, declared: "If you want to kill Christianity, you must abolish Sunday." So, in 1795 the committee decreed a new calendar in which each month would have three 10-day weeks (with five extra days at the end of the year). This eliminated Sundays and holidays (holy days), but after 10 years, the system was abolished. Animals had dropped dead in the fields from overwork, the system of commerce was a shambles, and people longed for the traditional system of religious observances.

In 1929, another atheistic government, the U.S.S.R., tried to abolish the seven-day week by decreeing a week of five days. This time the experiment lasted 11 years before the seven-day week was once again acknowledged.

It was God himself who set the precedent for rest. He provided for one day a week on which we would stop our work to rest, renew, and reflect. Jewish and Christian traditions call it the Sabbath. Jews rest on Saturday to commemorate creation and Christians rest on Sunday to commemorate the resurrection.

One of my newsletter subscribers reflected beautifully on this practice: "In knowing that our day of rest is coming at the end of each week, we are relieved of the heavy load we shoulder, holding fast to the Hope of rest that is to meet us."

Here are some strategies I use for maximizing my Sabbath rest:

*1. Worship.* I seek to know the God who made me. I express thanks for His mercies. Worship is a reminder that life is bigger than my own selfish desires. I try to express my enthusiasm for this to my children.

*2. Nap.* Everyone in our family takes a luxurious, guilt-free nap, though we are careful not to sleep so long as to disrupt sleep that night.

*3. Read.* I love reading biographies of heroes from history and learning from their examples how to live a more fruitful, productive life.

*4. Exeercise.* Our family loves to go kayaking or for a walk after Sunday naps. The fresh air, exercise and conversation bond us together as a family.

*5. Play.* We play by reading books, getting on the floor with the kids and exploring out of doors.

The important idea behind all of this is that God likes it when we get the rest we need. He made us that way from the very beginning.

## The Beginning Begins Now

Many people start down the path of leadership fitness, only to wear out and give up along the way. Don't be one of them! Remember: failure is God's way of giving you the fortitude you need to succeed. The great preacher F. W. Robertson said, "Forget mistakes; organize victories out of mistakes!"

In the follow-up exercise to this chapter, you'll have a chance to put some of your ideas into practice with a simple planning tool. Don't skip this step! Why not start moving today toward leadership success?

> "By perseverance the snail reached the ark."
>
> —Charles H. Spurgeon

> "Walk in wisdom toward outsiders, making the most of the time."
>
> —Colossians 4:5

# Consider This

Take a few minutes, and jot down answers to these questions. They will help you discover ways to keep yourself fit as a leader.

> "But as for you, keep a clear head about everything, endure hardship, do the work of an evangelist, fulfill your ministry."
>
> —2 Timothy 4:5

- Surveys tell us that we live among a very "stressed out" generation. The fast pace of life combined with uncertainty about the future and a lack of solid values is causing "burn out" at earlier ages than ever before. Have you ever experienced burn out? What caused it? What did you do about it?

- "Endurance" means the ability to stand pain, distress and fatigue. What do people who exhibit great endurance do differently?

> "For I am already being poured out as a drink offering, and the time for my departure is close. I have fought the good fight, I have finished the race, I have kept the faith. In the future, there is reserved for me the crown of righteousness, which the Lord, the righteous Judge, will give me on that day, and not only to me, but to all those who have loved His appearing."
>
> —2 Timothy 4:6-8

- Read 2 Timothy 4:5. What four things did the Apostle Paul tell Timothy to do during a time of great stress?

- Read 2 Timothy 4:6-8. What three things did the Apostle Paul claim with a clear conscience at the end of his life?

- What are some areas of life in which you are most prone to stress? What are some ways to develop equilibrium in those areas?

# Follow-Up Exercise

In the video, Dr. Myers said that the motivated person is not the one who has a constant state of high energy but the one who rises to the occasion, completes the task, and then returns to a balanced state.

**Hopefully, as you've read Chapter Four you picked up some new ideas to help you organize your time and regain lost energy. But true change requires planning. Take a few moments to plan some changes to which you will commit in the next three months?**

- **In the next week, I will...**

- **In the next month, I will...**

- **In the next three months, I will...**

Here's a simple planning tool you can use to put this pattern into practice. It involves four steps: Plan, Attack, Establish, Regroup. To employ this system, state your goal first.

**What is an important goal you would like to accomplish?**

Step 1— **Plan. In two minutes, describe the action you need to take to accomplish this goal (for example, "I will write a letter to my Congressional representative regarding an important issue I've been thinking about):**

Step 2— **Attack. Write down what you will do to aggressively act on your goal (for example, "I will rise at 6:30 tomorrow morning, accomplish my other tasks, and begin writing the letter at precisely 8:00 am, and work on it steadily for one hour."):**

"Remember to dedicate the Sabbath day: You are to labor six days and do all your work, but the seventh day is a Sabbath to the Lord your God. You must not do any work—you, your son or daughter, your male or female slave, your livestock, or the foreigner who is within your gates. For the Lord made the heavens and the earth, the sea, and everything in them in six days; then He rested on the seventh day. Therefore the Lord blessed the Sabbath day and delcared it holy."

—Exodus 20:8-11

**Step 3— Establish.** What factors could prevent you from following through on this goal (for example, "I could be distracted by checking e-mail, taking phone calls, or a lack of concentration.")?

**Step 4— Regroup.** What will you do to re-energize at the end of the task (for example, "I will treat myself to a cup of coffee or call a friend and encourage him or her to write a similar letter.")?

- **What will this effort help us do?**

- **What should this make us eager to do?**

**Read each of the two stories from history recounted below, and write your answer to this question: How did Squanto in the first story and the unknown man in the second story live out the principles of motivation discussed in Chapter Four?**

• When the Mayflower pilgrims landed, they were unprepared for the harsh conditions they were to face—nearly half the pilgrims died during the first winter. By God's grace, the remainder met Squanto, a Patuxet Indian who was the only survivor of a plague which had destroyed his tribe. Squanto had earlier been kidnapped and taken to Europe where he learned English and European customs. Upon encountering the pilgrims, he taught them to plant corn and find provisions. Squanto converted to Christianity, and according to Governor William Bradford of the Massachusetts Bay Colony, was "a special instrument sent of God for their good beyond their expectation." Because of Squanto, the colony survived and thrived, hastening the birth of a new nation, the United States of America.

"Teach us to number our days carefully so that we may develop wisdom in our hearts."

—Psalm 90:12

"If you do nothing in a difficult time, your strength is limited."

—Proverbs 24:10

• In 1876, Rutherford B. Hayes was elected President of the United States by one vote in the Electoral College. One of the Electoral College members was a congressman from Indiana who had been elected to the Electoral College by one vote. One man who voted for that particular Electoral College member had been sick on voting day but insisted that he be taken to the polling place anyway. Think of it: a president of the United States was elected by a sick man who was just stubborn enough to vote!

**Read the following Scripture passages in preparation for the next session: Psalm 90:12, Ephesians 5:15-16, 2 Timothy 4:5, Colossians 3:23 and Proverbs 24:10.**

"Pay careful attention, then, to how you walk—not as unwise people but as wise—making the most of the time, because the days are evil."

—Ephesians 5:15-16

"Then He told them, 'The Sabbath was made for man and not man for the Sabbath.'"

—Mark 2:27

## CHAPTER FIVE

# Planning for Victory

KEY QUOTE:
**The more vivid the goal, the more motivated people are to achieve it.**
**—Jeff Myers**

## CHAPTER AT A GLANCE

- Teach us to number our days.
- Each day is an investment.
- The tyranny of the urgent.
- Setting right goals rightly.
- The R.E.A.C.H. goal-setting strategy.
- The value of a strategic plan.

## Teach Us to Number Our Days

EVERY DAY IS AN INVESTMENT OF 24 HOURS that must be used wisely. It can never be reclaimed. You can invest wisely or poorly; but you cannot not invest. When you and I understand this and act accordingly, we grow wise. In Psalm 90:12 the psalmist prays, "Teach us to number our days carefully so that we may develop wisdom in our hearts."

Imagine that you have $27,375 to spend buying "important things" in life. Each item costs $9,125, so you can afford only three things from this list:

1. True love
2. Not having to worry about money
3. A sense of peace
4. Adventure
5. A position of power
6. Ability to make a difference
7. Attractiveness
8. Having lots of cool stuff
9. Opportunity to travel
10. Close walk with God
11. Living in a prestigious neighborhood
12. Popularity
13. Athletic talent
14. Being remembered as a great person after I'm gone
15. Having children who love the Lord

Which three would you choose?

_____  _____  _____

Which three would an impartial observer conclude are your top priorities judging by your current motivations and actions?

_____  _____  _____

## Each Day Is an Investment

Was it hard to select three things from the list above? Did you wonder what was behind the odd amounts of money? Imagine for a moment that instead of dollars you were spending days. The number 27,375 represents the average number of days in a person's life.

If you run out of money, you can always make more but not so with time. Even the most powerful and rich people in the world have only 24 hours in a day. Perhaps that's why the Apostle Paul taught, "Pay careful attention, then to how you walk—not as unwise people

but as wise—making the most of the time, because the days are evil" (Ephesians 5:15-16).

Once I showed the "important things" list to a group of students, and one of them said, "That's not fair! There are many good things on the list. Why can't I have them all?"

It is true that the items on the list are not necessarily mutually exclusive—God may bless you with many of them at one time. Still, I explained to the students in that group, the principle of scarcity says that you can never have everything you want—you have to make choices. It's true with money, and it's true with time as well.

## The Tyranny of the Urgent

For most people, the central problem is not that time is limited but that they make poor choices about how to invest the time they have. Some make poor choices about time by simply wasting it. In March 2005 the Kaiser Family Foundation released the results of a massive study on teens and media consumption which showed that the average American teen is engaged with media (television, computer, music) six hours a day. While there may be some value to media exposure, is it really worth six hours a day? That's time that cannot be used for developing relationships, honing skills, exercising, reading, or even resting. Once that time is wasted, it's gone forever.

The most startling aspect of the Kaiser study, however, wasn't that teens waste a lot of time. It's that they completely inundate themselves by using several kinds of media simultaneously. For example, teens don't replace old media (TV) with new media (computers, iPODs). Rather, they multi-task—instant messaging their friends while scouring the internet for homework research while listening to music with the television on. Where did teens learn that? Perhaps from parents who drive, talk on the phone, sip coffee, and listen to the radio at the same time?

> "Speak gently! 'tis a little thing Dropp'd in the heart's deep well; The good, the joy, that it may bring Eternity shall tell."
>
> —Attributed to G. W. Langford

> "Where thou art obliged to speak, be sure to speak the Truth: For Equivocation is half way to Lying, as Lying, the whole way to Hell."
>
> —William Penn

Everyone's looking for ways to make the most of their time, and a lot of us assume that efficiency can be gained by doing more than one thing at a time, and we're teaching our kids to do the same. But is it a valid assumption?

In 2001 Joshua Rubinstein studied what happens when people multi-task. He discovered that it actually wastes a lot of time, and in some cases—while driving, for example—it can be dangerous.

The heart of the problem isn't just that we waste time or try to do too many things at once. It's that our approach to the stewardship of time is entirely wrong. Years ago Charles Hummel wrote a much-reproduced booklet called *The Tyranny of the Urgent*. He pointed out that, rather than making time their servant, most people allow it to be their master. They go frantically from one urgent activity to the next and yet see very little progress. You see, it doesn't matter if you're using time efficiently if what you're doing is unimportant and irrelevant.

So what do world-changers do differently? In many cases they work a little harder and squeeze more out of the day. But the biggest difference between world-changers and everyone else is that they seek to get the *most important* things done right.

## Setting Right Goals Rightly

Setting goals can help you create change, remove self-imposed barriers, measure your progress, and become a better steward of your gifts. In this chapter, I'll expand on the video lesson in which I shared a simple goal-setting formula I use to focus on the most important things and get them done.

"Formulas" for goal-setting, though, generally are overrated. People tend to develop formulas that work for other people like themselves but leave the rest frustrated and feeling guilty that they aren't "goal-driven." I'm sensitive to that concern and hope you'll see that the following formula is simple, straight-forward,

and easy to apply. It works for all kinds of people. But before I share it, let's review why setting goals is so important in the first place:

*1. Setting goals adjusts your attitude for success.* The Apostle Paul wrote in 1 Corinthians 9 that we should "Run in such a way as to get the prize." I once heard that the medical definition of death is a body that does not change. We all desire change at some level, but very few people are satisfied with the results they are currently getting in life. If we don't have a big goal that's worth pursuing, greed and self-centeredness will likely propel us toward the wrong kind of change. God's desire isn't just that we avoid bad change, but that we pursue change that honors Him.

*2. Setting goals enhances your training.* The Apostle Paul wrote, "everyone who competes exercises self-control in everything." Athletes always train better when they're training for something. Some goals have natural deadlines. In a political campaign, for example, voting day is a deadline which approaches with urgency. But in many areas of life—child raising for example—creating deadlines where there are no natural deadlines forces you out of apathy into setting your sights higher than you would otherwise.

*3. Setting goals brings focus to activity.* The Apostle Paul wrote, "I do not run like one who runs aimlessly." That's a funny picture. What does it look like to run aimlessly? We all need markers to measure our progress. A runner, for example, strives to run his race in less time than he did six months before. A dieter seeks to have lower body fat than six months before, and a musician seeks to play with more skill and grace than she did the previous year. Setting out a marker gives you a better vantage point and brings focus to your activity.

*4. Setting goals instills self-discipline.* The Apostle Paul wrote, "I discipline my body and bring it under strict control." Self-discipline is necessary because most barriers to our success are self-imposed, and we must exert strength and character to break through them. To be sure, some of our limitations have been put in place by God to force us to rely on others. Other limitations have been put there by God to strengthen us as we seek to grow. As a result, wisdom is needed to discern the difference between the two. The goal-setting formula in this chapter takes this need for wisdom into account and shows how to incorporate wise counsel into your planning.

## The R.E.A.C.H. Goal-Setting Strategy

Remember the acronym "REACH" to walk yourself through a productive goal-setting process.

### R = Record. The key to achieving your goals is to write them down.

In one of His teachings about discipleship, Jesus used the example of well-thought-out goals to show how important it is to thoughtfully commit to God's plan:

> For which of you, wanting to build a tower, doesn't first sit down and calculate the cost to see if he has enough to complete it? Otherwise, after he has laid the foundation and cannot finish it, all the onlookers will begin to make fun of him, saying, "This man started to build and wasn't able to finish." Or what king, going to war against another king, will not first sit down and decide if he is able with 10,000 to oppose the one who comes against him with 20,000? (Luke 14:28-31)

The purpose of planning is that you've made your goal concrete—that is, you've set it forth and committed to pursing it heartily. Isaiah 32:8 says, "But a noble person plans noble things; he stands up for noble causes." Writing down your goals puts what would otherwise be random thoughts on paper where you can examine them, show them to others, and incorporate them into your actions.

When you write down a goal, you can look at it, adjust it, and tell others about it. This is truly as simple as it sounds:

- Get a piece of paper and write down three goals you want to accomplish within the next three months.
- Write quickly; spend no more than one minute on each goal.
- Write no more than one sentence each.
- When you finish, post your three goals where you will see them every day.

Don't let a change of heart stop you. If you change your mind during the time you're pursuing these goals, rewrite the goals and post the new ones. But keep them current, and keep them in writing!

### E = Envision. Imagine the benefits you'll receive from completing the goal.

The second step in good goal-setting is to envision the benefits. Often when I teach this goal-setting formula, my students balk at this step. Many feel it is self-indulgent and frivolous to dream about the good that will happen when they achieve their goals. While I understand their point, I strongly disagree with the conclusion. Remember the principles about vision in Chapter Two? That's what envisioning is—getting an inspirational picture of your vision, something that drives you forward.

Two days before writing this chapter, I was privileged to spend a couple of hours with a highly-regarded ministry leader I have known and admired for more than 20 years. This man has influenced millions, and although he's older now, he's as energetic and sharp as any man half his age. After sharing his vision for a significant goal, this man leaned across the table and said, "Jeff, I feel that my entire ministry up to this point has been preparation for what is happening now. The real ministry is just beginning!"

"Do you not know that the runners in a stadium all race, but only one receives the prize? Run in such a way that you may win. Now everyone who competes exercises self-control in everything. However, they do it to receive a perishable crown, but we an imperishable one. Therefore I do not run like one who runs aimlessly, or box like one who beats the air. Instead, I discipline my body and bring it under strict control, so that after preaching to others, I myself will not be disqualified."

—1 Corinthians 9:24-27

> "Listen, my son. Accept my words, and you will live many years. I am teachng you the way of wisdom; I am guiding you on straight paths. When you walk, your steps will not be hindered; when you run, you will not stumble. Hold on to instruction; don't let go. Guard it, for it is your life."
>
> —Proverbs 4:10-13

> "Go to the ant, you slacker! Observe its ways and become wise."
>
> – Proverbs 6:6

I left invigorated by this man's enthusiasm. He has cultivated the ability to describe in detail the benefits he imagines will result from accomplishing his goal.

When you fail to envision positive results, it's hard to believe the goals are worthwhile. Jim Collins, author of the bestselling business book *Good to Great*, encourages companies to set B.H.A.G.s ("big, hairy, audacious goals").[1] That's because the more vivid the goal, the more motivated people are to achieve it. The same is true for you personally. Imagine the awesome benefits of achieving your goal, and you will find it becoming a higher priority.

To envision the benefits of your goal, ask yourself, "How will this goal:

- help me live my gifts?
- strengthen my sense of purpose and meaning?
- create more security, adventure or freedom in my life?
- free me up to do what I really want to do?"

Write down at least 5 benefits of each goal you would like to achieve, and review them often.

### A = Act. Take the first step now, without hesitation.

The Bible tells us to look at the ant and become wise (Proverbs 6:6) because even ants prepare for the future. Here's an example that demonstrates the power of acting, even in small ways:

In 2005, at age 13, Johnny got the spending bug. He never spent a lot of money, but his allowance and some small earnings from mowing lawns gave him enough to play a couple of video games and buy soft drinks and candy bars, a couple of fast food meals, a movie ticket, and an occasional CD every week (at a total cost of about $30 per week). Without even realizing it, by the time Johnny graduated from

college at age 22, he had spent more than $15,600 on "stuff." He continued this kind of spending even after he had a good job, and by age 65 had spent $81,120.

How much money would Johnny have if he had:

- Saved just half that amount ($15 a week) and invested it in a mutual fund (earning an average of 12% interest) until graduating from college at age 22?
    Answer: More than $15,000

- If he had continued to save $15 per week until his retirement at age 65?
    Answer: More than two million dollars!

Can you imagine that? Even small actions that seem merely symbolic make a big difference through time.

Forceful action isn't just for leaders. It's for all Christians. We are to trust in God and act on that trust. When Nehemiah's enemies threatened to attack the city wall he was rebuilding, he rallied his troops saying, "Don't be afraid of them. Remember the great and awe-inspiring Lord, and fight for your countrymen, your sons and daughters, your wives and homes" (Nehemiah 4:14). Remember the Lord *and* fight. Part of obedience to God is acting on what we know to be right.

We should always be ready for action. Jesus told his followers, "Be ready for service and have your lamps lit" (Luke 12:35). Peter echoed this to his disciples: "[G]et your minds ready for action" (1 Peter 1:13). James even warned, "[F]or the person who knows to do good and doesn't do it, it is a sin" (James 4:17).

No matter your goal, act on it *now*—intentionally and with determination. Don't be like those who talk big but never do anything. Even small, symbolic steps make a difference because they set you on the right path.

## C = Consult. Seek the counsel of experts to gain clarity regarding your goals and increase your chances of of reaching them.

As I mentioned in Chapter Three, Gregg Harris taught me to "seek the Solomons" in my life. Solomon was the wisest man who ever lived. When the Queen of Sheba heard about him, she traveled to meet him and ask him all of her hard questions.

Seeking the Solomons who can advise me has helped me more than I can possibly describe to you, and I've taught it to thousands. When you set a goal, you may not have the information or education you need to achieve it, but others *do* have that knowledge and spending even a few minutes with them can dramatically boost your efforts. For example:

- If you want to establish a personal budget, purchase some Dave Ramsey or Crown Financial Concepts materials which will take you through the process step by step.
- If you are wondering how to make good investments, ask a financially successful person to recommend a good broker.
- If your goal is to develop self-discipline, ask a pastor or respected person to hold you accountable.
- If you want to improve family relationships, arrange to spend time with someone who has successfully raised children.

"Seeking the Solomons" turns every encounter into a learning opportunity. The person sitting next to you on the bus may know of a good book that would help you. The parishoner sitting next to you in church may have great insight into a problem you're facing.

Here are some of the habits I have adopted in seeking Solomons:

- I take a notebook with me everywhere I go, to take notes from speakers, jot down ideas or quotes that I hear, and to journal important thoughts.
- Whenever I hear a speaker, I introduce myself to compliment the speaker on the presentation and ask questions about his or her work.
- I write down pressing questions with which I'm struggling and pray for opportunities to meet people who have the answers.

Remember, if you don't ask, the answer is always "no." And the best news? Seeking wise counsel doesn't require any training. You can start today.

## H = Hone. Adjust and fine-tune as you go.

Veteran military leaders will tell you that a battle plan only lasts a few minutes. Situations change rapidly in combat, and the tide turns toward the army that is most adept at changing quickly to meet new challenges.

One of my favorite biblical leaders is Nehemiah. I wrote about Nehemiah in my *Secrets of Everyday Leaders* video coaching course because of the leadership lessons we can learn from the guy who rebuilt the walls of Jerusalem. I recommend that you study the book of Nehemiah to learn how to overcome apathy and move people to action.

Nehemiah demonstrates the art of keeping your eye on the goal but being flexible in how to achieve it. This splendid leader did at least four specific things to hone his goal under seemingly impossible circumstances:

*1. He did his homework.* Nehemiah asked questions of those who had seen the wall, and formed a plan based on what they told him. Yet when the time came to begin the actual rebuilding, he took several days to travel around the wall and adjust his plan as needed.

*2. He responded to pressure by advancing rather than retreating.* Although Nehemiah had the support of the King, he was also threatened by several enemies from outside and from

---

*(1) Nehemiah did his homework:*

"I went out at night through the Valley Gate toward the Serpent's Well and The Dung Gate, and I inspected the walls of Jerusalem that had been groken down and its gates that had been destroyed by fire."

–Nehemiah 2:13

*(2) Nehemiah responded to pressure:*

"When Sanballat the Horonite, Tobiah the Ammonite official, and Geshem the Arab heard [about this], they mocked and despised us, and said, 'What is this you're doing? Are you rebelling against the king?'
I gave them this reply, 'The God of heaven is the One who will grant us sucess. We, His servants, will start building, but you have no share, right, or historic claim in Jerusalem.'"

–Nehemiah 2:19-20

within. But when faced with these challenges, Nehemiah didn't lower the bar, he raised it. He proposed rebuilding the wall in blitzkreig fashion, with everyone—men and women, rich and poor—pitching in.

*3. He identified and counted on different levels of support.* Nehemiah may have hoped that everyone would pitch in to rebuild the wall, but they didn't. So Nehemiah built his strategy around those he could count on—a dedicated core of enthusiastic followers. While these folks worked, Nehemiah also isolated those who were threatening and abusive, and he inspired lazy workers by putting them in charge of rebuilding the wall near their homes (a job they were motivated by fear to complete).

*4. He persevered through opposition.* When Nehemiah's enemies said they would attack the workers, Nehemiah adjusted his strategy by arming the workers, establishing a guard, and implementing an alarm system so that he could quickly mobilize a military response. Nehemiah's enemies were intimidated by his proactive thinking, and they backed off.

Here are some questions to help you hone your goals:

- Is this goal still relevant?
- Is the goal still worth pursuing?
- Does the work need to be slowed down or speeded up?
- Is there a way to go forward when we would otherwise be tempted to retreat?
- Are there barriers in the way that I need to tackle first?
- Is it time to turn parts of the goal over to others?
- Am I stuck? Who can help me get "unstuck"?

It is up to us to make plans, but God is the One who guides our steps (Proverbs 16:9). We should be forceful in our actions but always aware of God's higher purposes.

## The Value of a Strategic Plan

While all four breakthrough strategies—strategic vision, strategic mission, strategic motivation, and strategic plan—are important, it is the strategic plan that pulls them all together. That's because:

- Without a strategic plan, it is impossible to have a strategic vision. Jesus said, "[I]f the blind guide the blind, both will fall into a pit" (Matthew 15:14).
- Without a strategic plan, your strategic mission remains unfulfilled. "Delayed hope makes the heart sick, but fulfilled desire is a tree of life" (Proverbs 13:12).
- Without a strategic plan, strategic motivation can be negative and harmful. "Even zeal is not good without knowledge" (Proverbs 19:2).

Yet with a plan in place, your vision takes on an inspirational quality. You can see how your mission fits with the gifts and talents of others, and you gain the energy to endure for the long haul.

This chapter's Follow-Up Exercise guides you through how to begin the goal-setting process. Just think of a compelling goal you would like to set, and the questions will lead you step-by-step through the process of organizing your goal into a workable plan. I encourage you to begin right away!

# Consider This

Take a few minutes, and answer these questions to start your goal-setting process.

- **On what does the average person base his or her choices about how to spend time?**

- **On what should Christians base their choices about how to spend time?**

> "Now it pleased the Lord that Solomon had requested this. So God said to him, 'Because you have requested this and did not ask for long life or riches for yourself, or the death of your enemies, but you asked discernment for yourself to understand justice, I will therefore do what you have asked. I will give you a wise and understanding heart, so that there has never been anyone like you before and never will be again.'"
>
> —1 Kings 3:10-12

- **Do you know a person who uses his or her time wisely? How is his or her life different? What can you apply to your life from this person's example?**

> "'Everything is permissible,' but not everything is helpful. 'Everything is permissible,' but not everything builds up."
>
> —1 Corinthians 10:23

● In what areas of your life could you benefit from better planning?

● Have you ever set a goal and accomplished it? What difference did it make in your life?

● Make a list of things that stop most people from setting and accomplishing goals. How could you avoid these mistakes in your own life?

# Follow-Up Exercise

"If you fail to plan, you're planning to fail." And if you're going to plan, why not plan to win? This follow-up exercise walks you through the steps of strategically planning the successful accomplishment of a goal.

**Check the areas in your life where could you benefit from better planning:**

\_\_\_ **Reading my Bible regularly**

\_\_\_ **Using money more wisely**

\_\_\_ **Getting in shape**

\_\_\_ **Making better dating choices**

\_\_\_ **Saving and investing money**

\_\_\_ **Find work I can love**

\_\_\_ **Living for God**

\_\_\_ **Sharing my faith**

\_\_\_ **Improving relationships with others**

\_\_\_ **Having a better diet**

\_\_\_ **Having more positive activities with friends**

\_\_\_ **Using time more wisely**

\_\_\_ **Becoming informed about what's going on in the world**

\_\_\_ _____

\_\_\_ _____

\_\_\_ _____

**If you've never been the kind of person to set goals, take a few minutes to answer the following questions:**

• **What lies have I believed about myself in the past?**

• **What am I resisting?**

"Happy is the man who finds wisdom and who acquires understanding, for she is more profitable than silver, and her revenue is better than gold."

—Proverbs 3:13-14

- **Where have I limited myself?**

- **What was I unwilling to risk?**

- **Where have I held back?**

**It's** _____ **(write down the date 90 days from now). What has to have happened for me to feel extremely satisfied with my progress?**

**What are five areas in my life where I need to set goals and take purposeful action?**

1.

2.

3.

4.


5.


Select one of the goal areas from above, and work through the R.E.A.C.H. goal-setting process.

R = Record. Write down your goal. Describe the outcome you hope to achieve. (For example, "By next February I will have given four speeches to community organizations in our town.")

E = Envision. Write down the benefits of achieving this goal. How will things be different once you're successful? (For example, "If I give these speeches, I'll be able to communicate my passion to hundreds of people, I'll feel great about overcoming fear, and I'll begin developing the skills I need to persuade others.")

A = Act. Find a way to act forcefully on your goal, and act now—even if only in a small way. (For example, "I will order a resource today that can help boost my public speaking skill." By the way, I encourage you to check out my *Secrets of Great Communicators* course if this is actually your goal—it's designed specifically for this purpose.)

"What then are we to say about these things? If God is for us, who is against us?...No, in all these things we are more than victorious through Him who loved us."

—Romans 8:31,37


"Now everyone who competes exercises self-control in everything. However, they do it to receive a perishable crown, but we an imperishable one. Therefore I do not run like one who runs aimlessly, or box like one who beats the air."

—1 Corinthians 9:25-26

"Brothers, consider your calling: not many are wise from a human perspective, not many powerful, not many of noble birth. Instead, God has chosen the world's foolish things to shame the wise, and God has chosen the world's weak things to shame the strong. God has chosen the world's insignificant and despised things—the things viewed as nothing—so He might bring to nothing the things that are viewed as something, so that no one can boast in His presence."

—1 Corinthians 1:26-29

C = Consult. Write down some people or organizations you can turn to for help. Who can give instruction, encouragement, or wise counsel? Write down the skills and knowledge you will need in order to succeed. (For example, "I will need to know how to get an audience's attention. Pastor Johnson is good at that, so I'll ask him how he does it. I also need to research my speech topic so I have strong evidence for the need and solution I am presenting, and I need to find a credible way for people to act on what they know. Mrs. Wyndham is an effective leader who knows how to credibly move people to action—I'll ask her for some techniques.")

**H = Hone.** Write down a tentative plan of action and establish success benchmarks for making sure you accomplish your goal. There are two parts to this: enlist others to help you become successful, and create a follow-up mechanism that allows you to discern how things are going and to make adjustments. (For example, "I will ask Mr. Soccoro to call me in two weeks to see how my contacts with community organizations have been going. I will ask Mr. Kennedy to check back with me in one month to look at an outline of my speech. After my first speech, I will ask Mrs. Wyndham to spend half an hour with me talking about what worked well in my speech and what I should do differently.)

"No one should despise your youth; instead, you should be an example to the believers in speech, in conduct, in love, in faith, in purity."

—1 Timothy 4:12

"For God has not given us a spirit of fearfulness, but one of power, love, and sound judgment."

—2 Timothy 1:7

**Now, put a time-frame to your goal. I will take the following three actions in the next 48 hours:**

1.

2.

3.

**I will take the following actions within the next 10 days:**

•

•

•

**I will take the following actions within the next 30 days:**

•

•

•

**Read the following Scripture passages in preparation for the next session: 1 Corinthians 1:26-29, 1 Timothy 4:12, 2 Timothy 1:7, Romans 8:31, 37, 1 Corinthians 9:25-26**

# Going Over the Edge

---

---

## CHAPTER AT A GLANCE

- Satan hates you and has horrible plans for your life.
- What the Devil is up to.
- Satan and other costumed characters.
- Satan's four lies.
- Responding to Satan's lies.
- A time to really live.

---

## Satan Hates You and Has Horrible Plans for Your Life

SATAN WANTS TO DESTROY YOU, not because he cares about you personally, but because you have the potential to carry out God's plan for the world. Satan hates God's plan more than anything else, and if God's plan succeeds, Satan is history. Throughout the Bible Satan has tried to destroy God's plan—deceiving Adam and Eve in the garden, encouraging Saul to kill David (the Messiah was to come from the house of David!), and getting Herod to kill all the babies in Bethlehem in an attempt to destroy the Christ child.

---

What does the Bible say about Satan? Test your biblical literacy by circling either true or false for each of these questions:

1. The name "Satan" means "evil one."
True   False
2. Another name for Satan is Lucifer, which means "morning star."
True   False
3. Satan is easy to recognize since he is so ugly.
True   False
4. God has already given us everything we need to crush Satan.
True   False
5. Satan is the equal and opposite of Jesus.
True   False
6. Satan is competing with God for your affection and allegiance.
True   False
7. Satan tries to deceive us by getting us to do the opposite of what God wants us to do.
True   False

You'll find the answers to each of these questions throughout this chapter (or if you're impatient, you can find all the answers in one place on the last page of this chapter).

## What the Devil Is Up To

The name "Satan" means "destroyer," "spoiler," "accuser," and "hater." He's all of these things—against you! Satan is not competing with God for your affection and allegiance—he hates you and wants to destroy you, spoil your impact, and then boast over your destruction by accusing you before the heavenly Father.

If this is so, why don't we hear more about Satan's work and how to counteract it? The answer will astound you.

## Satan and Other Costumed Characters

According to surveys of teenagers by pollster George Barna, 65% of self-identified evangelical Christian teens do not believe in a literal Satan. I don't know what their parents believe, but I suspect the percentage is about the same. And I don't blame these young people, by the way. After all, their parents told them Santa Claus, the Easter Bunny, and the Tooth Fairy are real, and they were lying. Why should kids believe parents about the guy with the red suit and pitchfork?

My reasons for believing in Satan are not deeply theological. The Bible's references (including the statements of Jesus) are not in jest, so I take them seriously. But furthermore, belief in Satan seems logical. After all, for evil to be truly evil, it must be intentional. Unintentional bad acts may be inconvenient, even tragic, but we do not consider them evil. But if an act is intentional, it is because there is an intelligent *will* which intended it.

In addition, if evil really exists, it can only be because there is an ultimate standard against which we are measuring it; there is an "ultimate good" and we can know what evil is because it stands in opposition to that good. Evil need not be equivalent in power or will to the good, but it must *exist* for our ideas of good and evil to have any meaning beyond our personal preferences.

It all comes down to this. Evil either is real and is personified by an ultimate evil will, or it is an illusion—or at least beyond the control of any will and therefore not truly evil. The Bible calls this evil will the *serpent, Satan,* the *devil, Lucifer.* It is clearly *not* just a "force" or "dark side." It is a person or being.

The trickiest thing about Satan—and the thing that shows how profoundly important the Bible's concept of evil is—is that he does not appear as an ugly, horned beast. Isaiah 14:12 calls him the "morning star" and in 2 Corinthians 11:14, Paul says that he disguises himself as an angel of light. Evil does not always appear as the ugly opposite of good. It often appears as *the* good, lulling us into satisfaction with anything that falls short of the best. Satan isn't as interested in getting us to do the complete opposite of what God wants us to do as he is interested in getting us to *accept* his counterfeit plan of salvation and *reject* God's genuine plan.

## Satan's Four Lies

According to Revelation 12:10, Satan is before God day and night "accusing the brethren." Some day he will be thrown out and God will declare victory, but in the meantime there is a battle between good and evil that rages continually in the heavenly realms.

Though the battle goes on, we must never be under the impression that Satan is the equal and opposite of Jesus. First John 4:4 says that He who is in us (Jesus) is greater than he who is in the world (Satan). Jesus is one with God, while Satan is a created being—presumably a fallen angel.

Jesus referenced this spiritual battle when he warned Peter in Luke 22:31-32: "Simon, Simon, look out! Satan has asked to sift you like wheat. But I have prayed for you that your faith may not fail. And you, when you have turned back, strengthen your brothers."

We must be on guard against Satan. It's striking that later in life Peter did strengthen his brothers by his writing:

Be sober! Be on the alert! Your adversary the Devil is prowling around like a roaring lion, looking for anyone he can devour. Resist him, firm in the faith, knowing that the same sufferings are being experienced by your brothers in the world. (1 Peter 5:8-9)

What does it mean that Satan is the accuser of the brethren? It means he accuses you and me of sin before God's throne. But Satan clearly attacks us directly as well.

Satan wants to take you out. His messages to you are designed to deflate you, to make you stray off course, and to instill fear in your heart. Has your Spirit ever been weighed down with messages like those noted below?

- "You don't have enough clout."
- "No one will pay attention."
- "You'll be too afraid."
- "You're no match for me."

James 4:7 says, "[R]esist the Devil and he will flee from you. Draw near to God, and He will draw near to you." What we need, to continue to grow as world-changers, is a way to respond to Satan's attacks. Don't let the devil's advances stop you from doing what God desires. After all, Satan is already defeated! Romans 16:20 says that God will crush Satan underneath our feet.

But exactly how does this work? How do we reply authoritatively to Satan?

## Responding to Satan's Lies

You'll notice that each of these responses is based on specific passages of Scripture. We take our model from Jesus in Matthew 4. Satan tempted Jesus by quoting Scripture, twisting the words to suit his purposes. But Jesus didn't fight with clever responses or a strong will. Rather, he quoted Scripture right back to Satan.

Satan is a finite being. He does not have all power, nor can he be everywhere at once. When he attacks you with his four lies, remind him of how God's truth applies to each one.

### When Satan says "You don't have enough clout," remind him that your weakness is God's strength.

It is not our strength that causes us to prevail, but Christ's strength working in us. The Apostle Paul reminds us in many Scripture passages that God is strong in us when we are weak:

- Romans 8:26—"In the same way the Spirit also joins to help us in our weakness…"
- 1 Corinthians 15:43—"…sown in corruption, raised in incorruption; sown in dishonor, raised in glory; sown in weakness, raised in power…"

"You are from God, little children, and you have conquered them, because the One who is in you is greater than the one who is in the world."

—1 John 4:4

"Now since the children have flesh and blood in common, He also shared in these, so that through His death He might destroy the one holding the power of death—that is, the Devil—and free those who were held in slavery all their lives by the fear of death."

—Hebrews 2:14-15

**"If Christianity should happen to be true— that is to say, if God is the real God of the universe—then defending it may mean talking about anything and everything. Things can be irrelevant to the proposition that Christianity is false, but nothing can be irrelevant to the proposition that Christianity is true."**

—G. K. Chesterton

**"Shining morning star, how you have fallen from the heavens! You destroyer of nations, you have been cut down to the ground."**

—Isaiah 14:12

• 2 Corinthians 11:30—"If boasting is necessary, I will boast about my weaknesses."

• 2 Corinthians 12:9—"…My grace is sufficient for you, for power is perfected in weakness."

• 2 Corinthians 13:4—"…For we also are weak in Him, yet toward you we will live with Him by God's power."

• Philippians 4:13—"I am able to do all things through Him who strengthens me."

It is important that we develop a strong scriptural basis for responding to Satan's attacks. Not only that, but we should learn what Scripture says about who we are in Christ. Our real strength comes from being in Christ, not just from being opposed to Satan's schemes.

## When Satan says "No one will pay attention to you," don't be intimidated—set an example.

First Timothy 4:12 says that we should set "an example to the believers in speech, in conduct, in love, in faith in purity." That's a tall order. It means specifically that by watching our lives, other people should be able to figure out the right thing to do.

William Jennings Bryan was one who, in spite of withering personal attacks, set an example by standing for what he believed to be true. Bryan was a defender of the common man, proudly identifying with everyday people even when he himself held positions of great power. Though I do not agree with many of his political beliefs, I've always admired the way Bryan stood up for what he believed.

The college at which I teach, Bryan College, is named as a memorial to the man for one defining incident in his life. In 1925, after a lifetime of political office, speechmaking and writing, Bryan received a desperate telegram from some Christian leaders in the state of Tennessee: Our anti-evolution law is under attack by the American Civil Liberties Union. Clar-ence Darrow is coming here to make a mockery of Christians. Will you come defend us?[1]

Bryan had every reason to say no. He was secure in knowing he had done far more than any man should be expected to do to stand for truth and justice. He was widely admired. He was spending his semi-retirement years in Florida, where Bryan's weekly Sunday school class numbered in the thousands.

Furthermore, Bryan did not support the Tennessee law, which stated that teachers were prohibited from teaching any view of the origin of man that contradicted the biblical account in Genesis. Bryan supported what the law was attempting to achieve, but he believed the law itself was faulty and unjust because of the way it punished teachers.

Still, Bryan agreed to go to Tennessee. He couldn't stand the thought of a sarcastic agnostic like Darrow mocking Scripture. Someone would have to take a stand against the dangerous doctrine of evolution, which Bryan believed led to injustice and oppression (this turned out to be prophetic—Marxist and fascist governments, rooting their philosophies in the "science" of evolution, made the 20th century the bloodiest century in all of human history).

Bryan traveled by train to the tiny burg of Dayton, Tennessee. Bryan's side won the day in the "Scopes Monkey Trial," but Bryan was pilloried in the press as a buffoon. He died a few days after the conclusion of the case, never having the opportunity to rebut his critics.

Was it a tragedy that Bryan went down in history this way? I don't believe even Bryan himself would think so. Just before he died, he said, "The humblest citizen in all the land, clad in the armor of a righteous cause, is stronger than all the hosts of error."[2]

It pleases God when we obey Him and surrender the outcome to Him alone. Today, tens of thousands of Christians around the world have taken up the cause to defend the truth of Scripture. Books, training programs, college courses, and other resources equip Christians to gracefully speak the truth in love. In spite of the billions of dollars invested and the shrewd calculations of Secular Humanists, the vast majority of Americans still believe in God and think that God created the world.

So what should be our response to the evils around us? Now is not the time to quake in fear, but to commit to bold action. We are to act boldly and cry out to God to root out evil and restore justice. Many of the prayers in the Bible are called "imprecatory prayers," meaning that they implore God to act justly and restore His good name. This seems harsh and unloving at first, but all good laws are based on what John Calvin called the "perpetual rule of love," the love of truth, of justice, of humanity, and of peace. The enemies of such laws must be stopped when they attack that which is worth loving in society.

## When Satan says "You're too afraid," remind him God has given you boldness.

The story of Christianity is not the story of man reaching out to God, but of God reaching out to man. And what's more, it's a family story—we have been adopted by our heavenly father and have earned the right to call him "Abba" or "Daddy."

Even if we meditate on that fact every day for the rest of our lives, I still don't think we would appreciate the full impact of what it means. If you are of the household of faith, you are a child of Almighty God, the Maker of heaven and earth. Scripture is clear about this:

- John 1:12—"But to all who did receive Him, He gave them the right to be children of God."
- Romans 8:16-17—"The Spirit Himself testifies together with our spirit that we are God's children, and if children, also heirs—heirs of God and co-heirs with Christ—seeing that we suffer with Him so that we may also be glorified with Him."

- 1 John 5:18—"We know that everyone who has been born of God does not sin, but the One who is born of God keeps him, and the evil one does not touch him."

What does this have to do with boldness? Simply that you don't represent yourself. You are backed by the power of Almighty God. As a child of the heavenly King, you have the right to enter His throne room. Satan may rail and accuse you all day long, but just walk right past him and curl up in your heavenly Daddy's lap.

Bottom line? When Satan accuses you, remind him you are a child of the King.

## When Satan says "You're no match for me," remind him your victory is assured.

When I feel weak as a leader, I often meditate on the Psalms. Here are some of my favorites that remind me of God's power and assure me that He will prevail:

- Psalm 8:1—"Lord, our Lord, how magnificent is Your name throughout the earth!"
- Psalm 11:4—"The Lord is in His holy temple."
- Psalm 16:1,10—"Protect me, God, for I take refuge in You....For You will not abandon me to Sheol."
- Psalm 20:7—"Some take pride in a chariot, and others in horses, but we take pride in the name of the Lord our God."
- Psalm 30:1—"I will exalt you, Lord, because You have lifted me up."
- Psalm 34:4—"I sought the Lord, and He answered me and delivered me from all my fears."
- Psalm 54:3-4—"For strangers rise up against me, and violent men seek my life. They have no regard for God. God is my helper; the Lord is the sustainer of my life."

"I was early brought to the living reflection that there was nothing in the arms of this man, however there might be in others, to rely upon for such difficulties, and that without the direct assistance of the Almighty I was certain of failing. I sincerely wish that I was a more devoted man than I am. Sometimes in my difficulties I have been driven to the last resort to say God is still my only hope. It is still all the world to me.""

—Abraham Lincoln

"And no wonder! For Satan himself is disguised as an angel of light."

—2 Corinthians 11:14

• Psalm 91:1—"The one who lives under the protection of the Most High dwells in the shadow of the Almighty."

You see, God has secured the victory. This drives Satan to the brink of madness, and He will do everything He can to persuade us otherwise, but stand firm! The victory is yours when the battle is the Lord's! (Proverbs 21:31).

## A Time to Really Live

I hope that as you've studied *Secrets of World Changers* you've gotten the strong impression that your life is not your own, that you are bought with a price. We all belong to God, and it is His glory we seek. When we adopt that perspective, the seeds of world-changing leadership grow rapidly in our lives.

But almost as if to challenge our convictions, we still wake up each day in a world caught up in self-worship. Thirty-four years ago Archibald McLeish wrote a chillingly prophetic article in the *Saturday Review* in which he described what happens when a society turns away from God and begins worshiping self:

There is, in truth, a terror in the world....Under the hum of the miraculous machines and the ceaseless publications of the brilliant physicists a silence waits and listens and is heard.

It is the silence of apprehension. We do not trust our time, and the reason we do not trust our time is because it is we who have made the time, and we do not trust ourselves. We have played the hero's part, mastered the monsters, accomplished the labors, become gods—and we do not trust ourselves as gods. We know what we are.

In the old days when the gods were someone else, the knowledge of what we are did not frighten us. There were Furies to pursue the Hitlers, and Athenas to restore the truth. But now that we are

gods ourselves we bear the knowledge for ourselves. Like that old Greek hero who learned when all the labors had been accomplished that it was he himself who had killed his son.[3]

The central irony of our day is that we know deep down our self-worship is in vain. Yet instead of repenting and returning to God, entire civilizations seem to be spinning further out of control.

Some people look around at the mess we're in and see the signs of the end times—that Christ is coming back soon. In Scripture, "end times" is a term which serves both as a warning of the coming judgment and an admonishment to believers to live wisely. This is made clear in passages such as 1 Peter 4:7-11:

Now the end of all things is near; therefore, be clear-headed and disciplined for prayer. Above all, keep your love for one another at full strength, since love covers a multitude of sins. Be hospitable to one another without complaining. Based on the gift they have received, everyone should use it to serve others, as good managers of the varied grace of God. If anyone speaks, his speech should be like the oracles of God; if anyone serves, his service should be from the strength God provides, so that in everything God may be glorified through Jesus Christ.

We cannot know when Christ will return, but we can follow Peter's teaching by:

• being clear-headed
• being disciplined and focused on God
• loving others deeply
• being hospitable (developing a strong sense of community)
• using our gifts to serve others
• administering God's grace
• speak only what is of God
• serving from the strength God provides.

No matter God's plan for the future, we can be world-changers if we obey Him. Everything that happens is an opportunity to spread God's kingdom message in the most practical way possible—by being agents of mercy and compassion to a world afflicted by the consequences of sin.

Not only that, but we should never give up the business of proclaiming the Lordship of Christ in every area of life. Abraham Kuiper, the great theologian and Dutch prime minister said, "There is not one square inch of the entire creation about which Jesus Christ does not cry, 'This is mine!'"[4]

Every institution on the planet—government, the church, the family, education, the media, the arts—has been affected by sin and is in need of redemption. We are to live as if each day matters for eternity (because it does) and as if we intend for our impact to extend across many generations. A good question to ask yourself is: Am I doing today what would make my great, great, grandchildren proud?

We opened this book by asking what history would write about us. Will those who write it say that during a time of great crisis we failed to act, or will they gratefully acknowledge that against all hope we stood firm to the very end? Make sure that your life will make them grateful.

"Men wanted for hazardous journey. Small wages, bitter cold, long months of complete darkness, constant danger, safe return doubtful. Honor and recognition in case of success."

—Ernest Shacketon's newspaper advertisement for a team to explore Antarctica

"You are from God, little children, and you have conquered them, because the One who is in you is greater than the one who is in the world."

—1 John 4:4

"The God of peace will soon crush Satan under your feet. The grace of our Lord Jesus be with you."

—Romans 16:20

> "To know that love is of God and to enter into the secret place leaning upon the arm of the Beloved—this and only this can cast out fear. Let a man become convinced that nothing can harm him and instantly for him all fear goes out of the universe. The nervous reflex, the natural revulsion to physical pain may be felt sometimes, but the deep torment of fear is gone forever. God is love and God is sovereign. His love disposes him to desire our everlasting welfare and His sovereignty enables him to secure it."
>
> —A. W. Tozer

# Consider This

Push yourself "over the edge" with these questions.

● Dr. Myers says in the video that Satan's goal is to destroy your effectiveness as a world-changer. Is it possible to identify Satan's work in order to counteract it?

● What are some examples from our culture which illustrate Satan's devious work?

● What are some of the obstacles you will face as you seek to make a difference in the world? What steps can you take to overcome those obstacles?

● In William Shakespeare's play *Henry the Fifth*, King Henry's famous St. Crispen's Day Speech says:

> We few, we happy few, we band of brothers;
>
> For he today that sheds his blood with me
>
> Shall be my brother...

Who are the people with whom you can band together to encourage one another and hold one another accountable as you develop as world-changers?

"A horse is prepared for the day of battle, but victory comes from the Lord."

—Proverbs 21:31

"Be sober! Be on the alert! Your adversary the Devil is prowling around like a roaring lion, looking for anyone he can devour."

—1 Peter 5:8

"But I fear that, as the serpent deceived Eve by his cunning, your minds may be corrupted from a complete and pure devotion to Christ. "

—2 Corinthians 11:3

And no wonder! For Satan himself is disguised as an angel of light. "

—2 Corinthians 11:14

● What are some practical ways you intend to apply the lessons you've learned from this study?

"When he [Satan] tells a lie, he speaks from his own nature, because he is a liar and the father of liars."

—John 8:44b

"He [Satan] was a murderer from the beginning and has not stood in the truth, because there is no truth in him."

—John 8:44a

# Follow-Up Exercise

The Bible presents Satan as a real being who willfully causes evil and whose intent is to destroy God's work of creation and redemption. In order to understand this enemy of our souls, let's take a few moments to examine his characteristics.

When law enforcement officers are trying to catch a criminal, they often create a "profile" of the type of person who commits crimes in order to narrow and expedite the search. I've noted below the known profile of a serial killer, a person who stalks and kills more than one victim. Look up the verses about Satan (evil one, devil, Lucifer, serpent) to see how his description compares to this profile of a serial killer.

**Serial Killer**

- Pre-crime stress—something that happens before the crime which motivates the killer: a quarrel, rage, insult or jealousy.
(Isaiah 14:12)

- The killer kills to exercise revenge or gain power.
(Matthew 4:8-9)

- The killer does not care about his victims and simply chooses them at random.
(1 Peter 5:8)

- The killer often captures his victims by conning them and putting them at ease.
(2 Corinthians 11:3)

- The killer puts on the appearance of being normal and even attractive.
(2 Corinthians 11:14)

- The killer is a convincing liar, often the last person his neighbors and friends would suspect.
(John 8:44b)

- Once the killer starts killing, he will not stop until he is made to stop.
(John 8:44a)

Plainly, you have an enemy who wants to sift, devour, deceive, and crush you in order to prevent you from becoming a leader who will make a difference for Jesus Christ. But how will he attempt to destroy you? What are you on guard against? Let's take a look at what seem to be Satan's four favorite stratagies:

Strategy #1: To deceive you. To deceive means "to make a person believe what is not true." Satan tries to deceive Christians by promising an "easier" way to get the good things God has promised. He mimicks God's good gifts with counterfeits. A counterfeit is an imitation of a thing which defraud by passing an imitation off as the original (to defraud means to "cheat out of"). Satan always has an

> "Then the woman saw that the tree was good for food and delightful to look at, and that it was desirable for obtaining wisdom. So she took some of its fruit and ate it; she also gave some to her husband, who was with her, and he ate it."
>
> —Genesis 3:6

"For I fear that perhaps when I come I will not find you to be what I want, and I may not be found by you to be what you want; there may be quarreling, jealousy, outbursts of anger, selfish ambitions, slander, gossip, arrogance, and disorder. I fear that when I come my God will again humiliate me in your presence, and I will grieve for many who sinned before and have not repented of the uncleanness, sexual immorality, and promiscuity they practiced."

—2 Corinthians 12:20-21

easier way, but it cheats you out of the blessing that God intends you to have by doing it His way.

For an example of Satan's counterfeit plan, read Genesis 3:6. What did the serpent lead Eve to believe she would gain by eating the fruit (besides food)?

Is this a good thing? ___ Yes ___ No

But what happened when Adam and Eve agreed to Satan's plan?

Think of some good things God wants us to have and how Satan tempts us to accept a counterfeit plan.

**Strategy #2:** To demoralize you. To demoralize means "to corrupt or undermine the morals of." Satan wants to demoralize you so you will feel guilty and withdraw from fellowship. If Satan can ruin your reputation, all the better—it will make non-believers think the church is full of hypocrites.

Have you ever had your morals corrupted or undermined? How did this affect your relationship with God and with other Christians?

> "No one should despise your youth; instead, you should be an example to the believers in speech, in conduct, in love, in faith, in purity."
>
> —1 Timothy 4:12

> "Be angry and do not sin. Don't let the sun go down on your anger, and don't give the Devil an opportunity."
>
> —Ephesians 4:26-27

According to 2 Corinthians 12:20-21, what are some ways Satan tries to corrupt believers and undermine the cause of Christ?

Look at 1 Timothy 4:12 to see how God wants you to respond when demoralized.

> "And let us be concerned about one another in order to promote love and good works, not staying away from our meetings, as some habitually do, but encouraging each other, and all the more as you see the day drawing near."
>
> —Hebrews 10:24-25

**Strategy #3:** To divide you. To divide means "to become disunited." When a wolf attacks a flock of sheep, it goes after the ones that are sick, simple (unaware), and separated. Those separated from the group are easiest to catch because they don't have the other bodies around for protection. If Satan can isolate you from other Christians, you will be easier for him to attack. Look up the following verses to see three ways Christians can be isolated from each other and thus vulnerable to Satan.

- Ephesians 4:26-27

> But our presentable parts have no need of clothing. Instead, God has put the body together, giving greater honor to the less honorable, so that there would be no division in the body, but that the members would have the same concern for each other. So if one member suffers, all the members suffer with it; if one member is honored, all the members rejoice with it."
>
> —1 Corinthians 12:24-26

- Hebrews 10:24-25

- 1 Corinthians 12:24-26

The word "accountability" is used to describe the strategy for sticking together to help one fend off Satan's attacks. Accountability means "being able to give an account of your actions, attitudes, words and motives to others." Look at the following verses to see what the Bible says about it.

- Ecclesiastes 4:12

- Proverbs 11:14

**Strategy #4:** To distract you. To distract means to "pull in different directions." During the Gulf War, General Norman Schwartzkopf and his aides designed a strategy in which they would make the enemy believe U. S. forces would attack at one particular place when they were actually planning to make a major assault in another location. The Iraqi army was distracted by the decoy and was completely unprepared when the attack came. They were neutralized, their weapons and preparation rendered ineffective, their forces paralyzed, and large portions of their arsenal were destroyed. Soldiers who have been neutralized actually hinder their army's objectives because they get in the way and destroy the motivation of the remaining troops.

What are some ways that Satan might distract Christians today?

"And if somebody overpowers one person, two can resist him. A cord of three strands is not easily broken."

—Ecclesiastes 4:12

"Without guidance, people fall, but with many counselors there is deliverance."

—Proverbs 11:14

Look up James 4:7 to see how to avoid being distracted.

> "Therefore, submit to God. But resist the Devil, and he will flee from you."
>
> —James 4:7

> "You are from God, little children, and you have conquered them, because the One who is in you is greater than the one who is in the world."
>
> —1 John 4:4

> "Now since the children have flesh and blood in common, He also shared in these, so that through His death He might destroy the one holding the power of death—that is, the Devil—and free those who were held in slavery all their lives by the fear of death."
>
> —Hebrews 2:14-15

Answers to the quiz in the opening section of Chapter Six:

1. The name "Satan" means "evil one"—false—Satan means "destroyer," "spoiler," "accuser" and "hater." 2. Another name for Satan is Lucifer, which means "morning star"—true—see Isaiah 14:12. 3. Satan is easy to recognize since he is so ugly—false—according to 2 Corinthians 11:14, Satan disguises himself as something good, an angel of light. 4. God has already given us everything we need to crush Satan—true—Romans 16:20 says that God will crush Satan under our feet. 5. Satan is the equal and opposite of Jesus—false—1 John 4:4 says that the one who is in us (Jesus) is greater than the one who is in the world (Satan). Jesus came to destroy the work of Satan according to Hebrews 2:14-15. 6. Satan is competing with God for your affection and allegiance—false—Satan does not care about your affection and allegiance. In fact, he hates you and wants to devour you. But he does want you to stop serving God. 7. Satan tries to deceive us by getting us to do the opposite of what God wants us to do—false—Satan wants us to stop short of doing what God wants us to do by getting us to accept his counterfeit plan. See Genesis 3:1-6 and Matthew 4:1-11.

Genesis 3:1-6

Now the serpent was the most cunning of all the wild animals that the Lord God had made. He said to the woman, "Did God really say, 'You can't eat from any tree in the garden'?"

The woman said to the serpent, "We may eat the fruit from the trees in the garden. But about the fruit of the tree in the middle of the garden, God said, 'You must not eat it or touch it, or you will die.'"

"No! You will not die," the serpent said to the woman. "In fact, God knows that when you eat it your eyes will be opened and you will be like God, knowing good and evil." Then the woman saw that the tree was good for food and delightful to look at, and that it was desirable for obtaining wisdom. So she took some of its fruit and ate it; she also gave some to her husband, who was with her, and he ate it.

Matthew 4:1-11

Then Jesus was led up by the Spirit into the wilderness to be tempted by the Devil. After He had fasted 40 days and 40 nights, He was hungry. Then the tempter approached Him and said, "If You are the Son of God, tell these stones to become bread."

But He answered, "It is written: 'Man must not live on bread alone but on every word that comes from the mouth of God.'"

Then the Devil took Him to the holy city, had Him stand on the pinnacle of the temple, and said to Him, "If You are the Son of God, throw Yourself down. For it is written: 'He will give His angels order concerning you, and they will support you with their hands so that you will not strike your foot against a stone.'"

Jesus told him, "It is also written: 'Do not test the Lord your God.'"

Again, the Devil took Him to a very high mountain and showed Him all the kingdoms of the world and their splendor. And he said to Him, "I will give You all these things if You will fall down and worship me.'"

Then Jesus told him, "Go away, Satan! For it is written: 'Worship the Lord your God, and serve only Him.'"

Then the Devil left Him, and immediately angels came and began to serve Him.

ENDNOTES

## Chapter Two

1. Timothy Harper, "The Stargazer," *Winnipeg Free Press*, July 29, 2004.

2. *The MacArthur New Testament Commentary Matthew 1-7* (Chicago: Moody Publishers, 1985), p. 239.

3. Alexis de Tocqueville, *Democracy in America*, trans. by George Lawrence, J. P. Mayer, ed. (New York: Harper Perennial, 1969), p. 465.

4. *The Confessions of Saint Augustine, Book 13*, trans. by Edward B. Pusey (New York: The Modern Library, 1999), pp. 317-8.

## Chapter Three

1. C. S. Lewis, *The Weight of Glory* (San Francisco: HarperCollins, 1949), p. 26.

## Chapter Four

1. Eston Dunn, "How to Sleep Better, Feel Great!" www.efitness.com.

## Chapter Five

1. Jim Collins, Good to Great (San Francisco: Harper Business, 2001).

## Chapter Six

1. You can learn more about the truth of what happended in the Scopes trial, as well as the current battles over creation, evolution, and Intelligent Design by reading *Monkey Business* by Marvin Olasky and John Perry (Nashville: Broadman & Holman Publishers, 2005).

2. William Jennings Bryan, "Cross of Gold Speech," in *Three Centuries of American Rhetorical Discourse*, Ronald F. Reid, ed. (Prospect Heights, IL: Waveland), p. 601.

3, Ravi Zacharias, *Can Man Live Without God?*, p. 54.

4. Quoted in Richard Mouw, *Uncommon Decency* (Downer's Grove, IL: InterVarsity Press, 1992).